Don't Get Burned on eBay

Don't Get Burned on eBay

Shauna Wright

O'REILLY®

Beijing · Cambridge · Farnham · Köln · Sebastopol · Tokyo

Don't Get Burned on eBay
by Shauna Wright

Published by O'Reilly Media, Inc., 1005 Gravenstein Highway North, Sebastopol, CA 95472.

O'Reilly books may be purchased for educational, business, or sales promotional use. Online editions are also available for most titles (*safari.oreilly.com*). For more information, contact our corporate/institutional sales department: (800) 998-9938 or *corporate@oreilly.com*.

Editor: Michele Filshie	**Cover Designer:** Mike Kohnke
Production Editor: Colleen Gorman	**Digital Artist:** Suzy Wiviott
Proofreader: Colleen Gorman	**Interior Designer:** David Futato
Indexer: Ellen Troutman	**Illustrators:** Robert Romano, Jessamyn Read, and Lesley Borash

Printing History:

March 2006:   First Edition.

ISBN: 0-596-10178-3
[LSI]   [2013-03-29]

Contents

Preface

Introduction

In early 2005, my friend Drue Miller and I received an email from Sarah Milstein, an O'Reilly editor. Through a convoluted series of contacts, she'd gotten our names as people qualified to write a different kind of eBay book—not a "how to" manual per se, but something combining personal stories with take-away lessons. Drue and I have a web site called WhoWouldBuyThat.com that had the voice Sarah was looking for. I believe the word used early on was "snarky." (Accurate, that.)

Drue's schedule ultimately didn't allow her to participate as an author (we snagged her later as a tech reviewer), but I was game. What followed were several conversations between Sarah and myself about what exactly we wanted this book to be—a book that's fun to read and extremely informative. That's what you'll find here.

The stories within this book are all true, recounted (usually on the message boards in eBay's Community section) by the people who experienced them. Minor artistic license has been taken where necessary, and all names have been changed to protect the innocent, the ignorant, and the guilty.

Audience for This Book

This book is for you if you have a working knowledge of eBay (just enough to get you in trouble if you don't know what to look out for). In this book, you'll get information in a way you'll remember—real stories about real people. After every story, I'll tell you how to avoid that situation or, if you're already neck-deep, escape it.

Even if you're a long-time eBayer, I'm fairly certain you'll come away from this book with a few nuggets of wisdom. As an example, I'm always amazed at the number of experienced sellers who routinely accept payments via PayPal yet don't know the policies PayPal has in place to protect them against fraud—until it's too late.

If you're new to eBay, this book is also for you. It may be a bit more advanced than you're ready for right now, but if you read it you'll avoid the traps many people fall into simply because they don't know any better. I certainly wish I'd known what's in these pages when I first stumbled onto eBay back in 1998!

Organization of This Book

This book is sometimes aimed at buyers and sometimes at sellers. Here's a brief overview of what's in the book:

Chapter 1, *Don't Get Burned on Bidding*
> This chapter gives you information about common bidding and communication errors, shill bidding, and bid histories.

Chapter 2, *Don't Get Burned on Payment*
> Chapter 2 walks you through PayPal's rules, Unpaid Item Disputes, money orders, and Western Union wire transfers.

Chapter 3, *Don't Get Burned on Packaging*
> This chapter talks about inadequate packaging (what packages to use, what not to use), and gives tips for where to find materials and when to use local pick-up.

Chapter 4, *Don't Get Burned on Shipping*
> In Chapter 4, learn about major U.S. shippers, international shipments, insurance, and customs.

Chapter 5, *Don't Get Burned by Other eBayers*
> Read about feedback, eBay's Seller Preferences, counterfeits, and selling for others.

Chapter 6, *Don't Get Burned by Scammers*
> Chapter 6 provides information about phishing, account take-overs, identity theft, escrow scams, and buyer scams.

Glossary
> There's a glossary at the end of the book which explains some of the terms I use throughout the book. Veteran eBayers will know them already, and while I don't want the eyes of anyone less-experienced to glaze over, I also don't want to spend a lot of time in the main text defining standard terms. Plenty of other tomes serve as a sort of "eBay 101," but that wasn't my goal here.

Conventions Used in This Book

The following typographical conventions are used in this book:

Italic
> Used for glossary terms when they first appear in a chapter.

`Constant width`
> Used for HTML tags.

Navigation
> Arrows are used to signify navigation paths; for example, Advanced Search → Members → Find Contact Information means that you should go to eBay, click Advanced Search, select Members, and then choose Find Contact Information.

We'd Like to Hear from You

Please address comments and questions concerning this book to the publisher:

O'Reilly Media, Inc.
1005 Gravenstein Highway North
Sebastopol, CA 95472
(800) 998-9938 (in the U.S. or Canada)
(707) 829-0515 (international/local)
(707) 829-0104 (fax)

To comment or ask technical questions about this book, send email to:

bookquestions@oreilly.com

We have a web site for the book, where we'll list examples, errata, and any plans for future editions. The site also includes a link to a forum where you can discuss the book with the author and other readers. You can access this site at:

http://www.oreilly.com/catalog/dgbebay

For more information about books, conferences, Resource Centers, and the O'Reilly Network, see the O'Reilly web site at:

http://www.oreilly.com

Safari Enabled

When you see a Safari® Enabled icon on the cover of your favorite technology book, that means the book is available online through the O'Reilly Network Safari Bookshelf.

Safari offers a solution that's better than e-books. It's a virtual library that lets you easily search thousands of top tech books, cut and paste code samples, download chapters, and find quick answers when you need the most accurate, current information. Try it for free at *http://safari.oreilly.com*.

Credits

Michele Filshie (editor) is the editor of four Personal Trainers (another O'Reilly series) and assistant editor for the Missing Manual series. Before turning to the world of computer-related books, Michele spent many happy years at Black Sparrow Press.

Drue Miller (technical reviewer) is a writer, designer, and avid collector of mid-century glassware, vintage clothing, and really bad clown art. Since 1998, Drue has bought and sold many items on eBay, both for herself and for others as an eBay "Trading Assistant." Drue was also the Director of Research at AuctionDrop, the first nationwide eBay drop-off service, where she developed internal processes and trained staff on the art of selling on eBay. She is also the co-creator of "Who Would Buy That?", a weblog of weird eBay auctions (*http://www.whowouldbuythat.com*). Drue lives in Pittsburgh with her husband.

David A. Karp (technical reviewer) has written 10 power-user books available in 9 languages, including the bestselling *eBay Hacks: Tips & Tools for Bidding, Buying, and Selling*. An eBay fanatic and a compulsive tinkerer, David served as the editor of *PayPal Hacks*, and has been spotted teaching classes at the last few eBay Live! conferences. Contact him at *ebayhacks.com*.

Acknowledgments

This book was written under the power of more 12-packs of Fresca than I can count, during many late nights with "The Daily Show" humming happily in the background (thank you, Jon Stewart). Frequent breaks were necessary to feed at least one of the four feline mouths in my home.

This is not my first writing project—I've been writing as long as I can remember—but it is my first book. I can now safely say it's not *nearly* as easy as it looks. I'll resist the urge to thank the academy, but there are some fabulous people to whom I owe my utmost gratitude.

To Sarah Milstein and Michele Filshie, my very kind and patient editors who (bonus!) get my twisted sense of humor. Without them I'm certain I wouldn't have been able to navigate this process successfully.

To the regulars on eBay's Answer Center boards, who gave me the knowledge that eventually became this book. They know more about eBay than most people will ever forget.

To my co-workers Kyle Alegrete, Joni Beyer, Ryan and Racquel Cosare, Debbie Garabato, Bryce Hatch, Carol Lussier, Esteban Tahmazian, and Daniel Van Belle, who keep me sane in an insane place and can always make me laugh (especially at myself).

To Pableaux Johnson, a many-time author and one of the funniest people I know, who for years has said, "You have a book in you. Write it."

To Charles Rhodes, who was first a neighbor, then a friend, and is now one of my closest confidants.

To Drue Miller, my long-time partner in crime with whom a series of late night emails sparked the idea for WhoWouldBuyThat.com.

To Leslie Harpold, my dearest friend and mentor, who truly believes I'm capable of anything if only I'd get up off my ass and do it.

To Tim Powell, the Ethel to my Lucy, who has seen me at my most insane and loves me in spite (or maybe because) of it.

To my parents, Patrick and Lienda Carter, who have always encouraged me to try everything (and are sure I'm good at it all).

And finally, to Mitch Herron, who for some reason has spent the better part of his life thinking I'm the most beautiful, brilliant woman in the world. May the spell never be broken.

1

Don't Get Burned on Bidding

Bidding on eBay is nothing short of an art form. Anyone who tells you otherwise should be informed his pants are on fire.

Contrary to popular belief, punching in some numbers isn't all there is to bidding. What should you look for when selecting a seller? Does bidding early have consequences? How can mistakes be corrected? Can you spot *shill bidding?* And how much *is* that doggie in the window?

There's a definite learning curve for the entire process, and people tend to make a lot of mistakes on the way up. Unfortunately, these mistakes aren't without consequence—they can cost you time, money, frustration, and possibly even your eBay account.

Oh, stop furrowing your brow (Botox is one of the few things you can't buy on eBay). I'm not going to let that happen to you. Forewarned is forearmed, as the saying goes.

Don't Act Like A Newbie

Entire tomes could be written about rookie mistakes on eBay, but who would read them? The *newbies* are too busy making the mistakes, and the veterans are too experienced to bother reading about them. Nevertheless, eBay policies can be very intricate and they manage to trip up both subsets of eBayers with alarming frequency.

Being Outbid Doesn't Mean You're Off the Hook

Lisa, an avid Beatles fan, ran across the holy grail of Fab Four collectibles—a tin of "Margo Of Mayfair" Beatles Bath Talc from 1964 in perfectly unblemished, mint condition (Figure 1-1). Lisa was so excited that she immediately placed several bids, even though the auction still had two days left. None of the bids were high enough to beat the current high bidder's *proxy*, so she dejectedly went back to browsing.

Lo and behold, someone else was selling the exact same thing and that auction had only a few minutes to go! Lisa jumped into the bidding fray and emerged triumphant.

The next day, she received a notice from eBay stating the *high bidder* on the first auction retracted his bid, putting Lisa in the lead, and the auction later closed with her as the winner. She was then on the hook to pay for both auctions (and contemplating a second job).

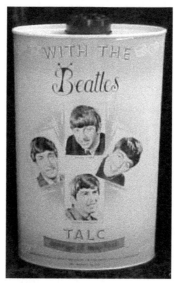

Figure 1-1. The hallowed "Margo of Mayfair" Beatles tin. Who knew 40-year-old powder could be so expensive? Buy two and they're even more expensive bookends!

Avoid it!

Lisa's colossal error was bidding on two identical items at the same time. All bids are live until the end of an auction, so bids retracted by another bidder or canceled by the seller can put you back in the lead.

When you see something you want to buy, add it to your *Watch List* (found on your *My eBay page*) and bid closer to the end of the auction. This gives you the chance to research it or browse for similar items without tying up your money waiting for an auction to close.

NOTE   Keep in mind that few items on eBay are so rare they won't show up again, so don't fall into a "now or never" trap. Search completed auctions on the *Advanced Search page* (linked from the top right of every eBay page) to see how many times something has been listed in the past 30 days, and how much it sold for.

If you find yourself in Lisa's situation and the second auction hasn't closed yet, you can always email the seller, explain what happened and ask him to cancel your bid. Keep in mind he doesn't have to acquiesce and may even refuse out of spite if he sees you've already won an identical item. Sellers don't like people treating bids as though they go into a "shopping cart" from which they can be removed later.

Escape it!

If you're the buyer, there's only one way out of this situation: beg for the seller's mercy.

Politely explain what happened and ask if he'd be willing to cancel the deal if you pay his *listing fees* (which vary depending on how the item was listed and its final selling price). He certainly isn't obligated to agree but if the auction attracted a lot of bids, he may be able to quickly sell the item to an *underbidder* through a *Second Chance Offer*.

But should the seller refuse to take pity on you, be prepared to either pay for the item or accept an *Unpaid Item Strike* (a few of those and eBay kicks you to the curb). You may also receive *negative feedback* from the seller.

NOTE   Of course, you can always get the item and then sell it yourself on eBay. More than a few items on the site are there because of a purchasing mistake!

Check and Double-Check Your Bids

Bob placed a bid on a Coach wallet he knew his wife had been coveting.

The starting bid was 99 cents so he entered a proxy of $10—at least, that's what he *thought* he entered. Later on he discovered he'd accidentally entered an extra zero, making his actual proxy $100.

A last-minute *bidding war* broke out between two other bidders, neither of whom outbid Bob's proxy, and the auction ended at $76. Bob's wife was thrilled at the good deal he got. He considered divorce, but quickly surmised it would be more expensive than the wallet for which he was obligated to pay.

Avoid it!

eBay's rules allow the buyer to retract a mistyped bid as long as the correct amount is immediately rebid. For details, go to Help → A to Z → R → Retracting a Bid (Figure 1-2). *Bid retractions* are also permitted if the seller's contact information is invalid or the item description significantly changes.

Retractions are *not* permitted if you just change your mind and no longer want the item. That, however, is a valid reason for divorce in most states. In case you were wondering.

Bid Retractions

Before bidding on an item on eBay, be sure to read the item description and check the seller's feedback. If you have any questions about the listing, contact the seller by going to the View Item page and clicking on either the seller's User ID or on the Ask Seller a Question link.

Please remember that every bid on eBay is binding (unless the item is listed in a category under the Non-Binding Bid Policy or the transaction is prohibited by law or by eBay's User Agreement). Bidding on multiple identical items should be done only if you intend to buy all of the items.

It is ONLY OK to retract a bid if...,

- You accidentally enter a wrong bid amount (for example, you bid $99.50 instead of $9.95). If this occurs, re-enter the correct bid amount immediately.
- The description of an item you have bid on has changed significantly.
- You cannot reach the seller. This means that you have tried calling the seller and the seller's phone number doesn't work, or you have tried emailing the seller and it comes back undeliverable.

Before you retract your bid, please read complete information on bid retractions including the Special Retraction Rules.

Item number of auction in question:
```
123456789
```

Your explanation of the retraction:
```
Entered wrong amount          ▼
```

If you have a valid reason not listed above, you can:
Contact the seller and ask the seller to cancel the bid, or contact Rules & Safety

```
Retract bid
```

Figure 1-2. This handy-dandy form lets you retract a bid if you have a reason eBay deems valid. Use it sparingly, if at all. The confirmation page you're shown when placing a bid is there for a reason, skippy.

Escape it!

Remember this: bidders *retract* bids, sellers *cancel* bids. Although there are very exacting rules for the former (see "The 12-Hour Rule" sidebar later in this chapter), a seller can cancel a bid at any time and for any reason she likes.

So if you find yourself in a position like Bob's, you can certainly email the seller, plead your case, and ask her to cancel your bid. Sellers hear all kinds of sob stories so she may not be willing to help you, but it's worth a shot.

Be sure to ask before the auction ends, as bids can't be canceled (or retracted, for that matter) afterwards.

The 12-Hour Rule

Bid shielding used to be a huge problem on eBay. It involved one person using two IDs to simulate a bidding war, which artificially raised the high bid on an auction and discouraged others from bidding. In the auction's final seconds, all the bids from one ID were retracted, leaving the other ID to win the auction at a very low price.

In response to the problem, eBay came up with extremely specific timing rules for retractions. If you place a bid *before* the final 12 hours of an auction, retracting that bid retracts *all* the bids you've placed on the item thus far.

If you bid *during* the final 12 hours of an auction, then you can retract only within one hour of placing the bid—and only that bid is retracted. Bids placed prior to the final 12 hours can't be retracted at all during the final 12 hours.

The 12-Hour Rule (as it's often called) also applies to sellers because auctions can be ended early only if they have more than 12 hours remaining. This keeps sellers from ending auctions at the last minute simply because bidding hasn't gone as high as they want.

It may seem like a complicated system, but the 12-Hour Rule has virtually eliminated both problems.

No One Wants You as a Penpal

Eden joined eBay and in her first week bid on multiple bottles of St. John's Wort. She was outbid at the last second—a practice known as *sniping*—on every auction.

She began sending nasty emails to the people who outbid her, accusing them of working with the seller—who must *surely* have known what her high proxy (maximum bid) was. After the other bidders reported her to eBay for misusing the mail forwarding system, Eden's account was suspended.

Avoid it!

While letting Eden win one of her auctions might have been in the interest of public safety, the *Contact Member* feature shouldn't be used by the buyer or seller for any purpose but the facilitation of a transaction. What Eden did is considered "harassment."

Furthermore, it's impossible to see another person's *hidden proxy* unless it's already been exceeded. Keep in mind that snipers aren't guaranteed to win. The highest bid always wins, no matter when it's placed (see "The Fine Art of Decoding Bid Histories" sidebar later in this chapter).

Escape it!

Depending on the violation that caused it, an *account suspension* may be temporary. It certainly doesn't benefit eBay to lose paying customers so they'll often try to work with you to get your account reinstated. If you want redemption, you'll do what's required.

The good news is that suspensions are rarely immediate or unforeseen. You'll get at least one email warning that details your offense and tells you to knock it off. Heed the warning and you'll be fine. Ignore it at your peril.

NOTE   Keep in mind you're *not* permitted to register a new ID or use another existing ID while you're suspended.

Monitor Your Spam Folder

Gene won an auction for a high-end bread machine. He immediately paid through *PayPal* and emailed the seller to ask when the item would be shipped. The seller didn't reply, so every few days Gene emailed her again.

By the time his item arrived two weeks later, Gene had already left *neutral feedback* for the seller complaining of poor communication

The Fine Art of Decoding Bid Histories

Newbies and veterans alike are often flummoxed by bid histories. eBay's method of showing what happened during an auction isn't intuitive, but with a little guidance you'll be able to decipher the complete blow-by-blow—and it'll make perfect sense. A few truisms to keep in mind:

Truism 1: eBay's bidding system doesn't make mistakes. Every single bid placed during an auction is archived on the *bid history* page as soon as it's successfully placed. No exceptions.

Many eBayers insist they've been involved in an auction where someone was able to hide a bid or to bid after an auction's close. Such assertions are always the result of misreading a bid history (oftentimes after being *sniped*). Like Elvis, "phantom bidders" are frequently spotted but no one has ever been able to prove their actual existence. But I like to pretend they'd also wear white jumpsuits.

Truism 2: Bid histories are ordered by amount, not by date. It's always important to note the *time and date stamp* on each bid.

People tend to cry "foul" (and other four-letter words) when they see a winning bid that was placed several days before any of the other bids. This anguish stems from the assumption that bids are ordered on the page in chronological order—which may sometimes be true, but usually isn't.

No matter when bids are placed, they're always listed from highest to lowest on the bid history page (with the exception of any canceled or retracted bids, which are always at the bottom of the page).

Truism 3: The proxy system doesn't show every time it bids. The proxy system is essentially the backbone of the bidding process on eBay. Put simply, it allows you to enter your absolute maximum bid whenever you like and then walk away from the computer, secure in the knowledge that eBay's bidding gnomes are hard at work raising your bid as necessary to keep you in the lead.

One telltale sign of a *winning proxy bid* is that it's dated earlier than the bids beneath it. Unlike bids placed manually (i.e., one at a time while you're at your computer), you *won't* see a time and date stamp every time the proxy system bids on your behalf. As long as you remain the high bidder, your name simply floats to the top of the bidding history, keeping its original timestamp.

—*continued*—

Now that you know the basics, let's break down a bidding history in detail. Take a look at Figure 1-3.

User ID	Bid Amount	Date of bid
creativemaggie (1146 ⭐)	US $28.00	Dec-18-05 09:59:54 PST
sabo1643 (65 ⭐)	US $27.00	Dec-21-05 19:36:57 PST
daslivs (74 ⭐)	US $25.00	Dec-20-05 17:25:56 PST
daslivs (74 ⭐)	US $23.00	Dec-20-05 17:25:44 PST
mlasky18 (-1)	US $20.00	Dec-18-05 16:39:56 PST

Figure 1-3. A typical bid history page on eBay. The dates and times may not make sense if you try to read them from top to bottom, but the bid amounts are always ordered from highest to lowest.

I'll convert the times shown into non-military to make things easier.

The seller set the starting bid for this auction at $18.99.

C placed the first bid. On December 18 at 9:59 a.m., she placed a proxy of $28.00. At that point, the auction page shows her as the high bidder, and the high bid as $18.99.

(Remember the proxy system uses only as much of a bid as necessary to keep someone in the lead, and at that point it didn't need more than $18.99 of C's bid for her to remain the top bidder since there were no other bidders.)

M bid at 4:39 p.m. the same day, December 18. He placed a proxy of $20.00. We know his proxy amount because it wasn't enough to take the lead. Now the auction page still shows C as the high bidder, and $20.50 as the high bid (M's proxy of $20 plus one bid increment, which at this bidding level is $0.50).

On December 20, D placed two bids at 5:25 p.m. The first bid was $23.00, and 12 seconds later he bid again, this time $25.00. Neither was enough to take the lead, so the auction page still shows C as the high bidder, and $26.00 as the high bid (D's highest proxy of $25 plus one bid increment, which at this bidding level is $1.00).

On December 21, S placed one bid at 7:36 p.m. He bid $27.00, which was not enough to beat C's earlier proxy.

—continued—

Now, what I want point out is that C won the auction even though four bids were placed *after* hers. That's the proxy system at work. Notice how the bid history doesn't have a separate time and date stamp every time the system bid on C's behalf—it just kept her ahead by one increment and floated her name to the top of the bidding list.

It definitely takes some practice to get the hang of reading bid histories correctly, but once you know how, you'll never again wonder how you won or lost an auction.

Just remember the Three Truisms—and you'll have this very handy skill mastered in no time.

and slow shipping. The seller in turn left him negative feedback and added him to her *Blocked Bidder list.*

Later on, Gene discovered his Internet service provider (ISP) had upgraded its *spam* filters and the seller *had* been replying to his emails—they were just stuck in his spam folder.

Avoid it!

There are several issues here.

First off, while communication is wonderful, it isn't required. Most eBay transactions take place without a word being exchanged between the buyer and seller. The buyer wins, the buyer pays, the seller ships. The end.

Should you prefer to do things differently, it's good to remember many ISPs are now filtering spam with the ferocity of a P. Diddy bodyguard. So when you're involved in an eBay transaction as the buyer or seller, it's important to check your spam folder frequently (or shut off those filters altogether).

You should also keep an eye on the Messages section of your My eBay page (Figure 1-4). Any notes sent to you within the eBay system show up there.

Figure 1-4. To make sure you're getting all your eBay-related email, be sure to check the Messages section of your My eBay page.

If you aren't getting replies to your emails, it's okay to use an antiquated device I call "the telephone" to reach your trading partner. You can usually get her number by going to Advanced Search → Members → Find Contact Information. This works only for recent transactions in which you were either the buyer or seller of record.

And finally, Federal Trade Commission law governing online sales allows a seller 30 days to ship an item after being paid unless the contract (in our case, the auction page) promises shipment sooner.

The vast majority of sellers send their items out much faster than the law requires, but shopping online isn't for the impatient. If you need something quickly for a special event, you should read the auction description carefully and if you don't see anything about shipping, contact the seller before you bid to make sure she can accommodate your wishes.

> **N O T E**   It's good to know FTC law and how it protects you
> when you're shopping online. The rules for "mail
> order" sales generally apply (find them at *http://www.
> ftc.gov/bcp/conline/pubs/buspubs/mailorder.htm*),
> but the FTC web site also has a page specifically for
> online auctions at *http://www.ftc.gov/bcp/conline/
> pubs/online/auctions.htm*. Be patient, polite, and flex-
> ible (when possible) and most of your transactions
> will go very smoothly.

Escape it!

Unfortunately, *feedback* is largely permanent. Gene can ask the seller
to go through *Mutual Feedback Withdrawal* (Help → A to Z → M →
Mutual Feedback Withdrawal) but the seller doesn't have to agree.

> **N O T E**   If the feedback someone leaves for you violates
> eBay's rules, it may qualify for complete removal. It's
> rare, but it happens. See Help → A to Z → F → Feed-
> back Removal for more details.

When Sellers Go Bad

At one point or another, nearly every eBay buyer has trouble with a
seller. While it appears buyers who break the rules are quickly repri-
manded, bad sellers seem to linger in perpetuity—rather like that
allergy you can't shake because your boss is too cheap to have the air
ducts purged of whatever biohazard is growing in them.

But unlike that situation, you *do* have a say in whether a lousy seller
stays or goes. And you don't even have to call OSHA.

Where's Tony Soprano When You Need Him?

Lance found a car he liked on eBay and placed a low bid. When the auction closed, he was delighted to find himself the winner. He got an amazing deal.

He excitedly emailed the seller, who refused to sell the car because the bidding didn't go as high as she thought it would. Lance was surprised to learn eBay can't force a seller to actually honor a high bid.

He left negative feedback (a.k.a. "*negging*") and vowed vengeance but the seller just laughed as she *negged* him back. She and Lance lived in different states... and how far could he get without a car?

Avoid it!

When the dotcom bubble burst a few years ago, eBay had to fire the goon squad that went around kneecapping sellers who didn't follow through on their transactions.

Now, a buyer's only recourse is to file a report against the seller for non-performance at *http://pages.ebay.com/help/policies/seller-non-performance.html*. eBay sends the seller a stern warning and if the behavior continues, they'll suspend the seller's account.

While leaving a neg may make you feel better in the short-term, eBay doesn't monitor feedback, so buyers' reports are the only way to make it known a seller is breaking the rules.

Escape it!

Aside from filing a non-performance report, there isn't much you can do as a buyer (unless, of course, you happen to have your own personal goon squad). You may be able to avoid getting a neg if you don't give one but that's kind of a wussy way to handle things.

Having said that, newbies are especially protective of their feed-back—and for good reason. Someone who's received only a few feedbacks will see his overall positive percentage plummet with a single neg, while the impact is much less for someone with thousands of feedbacks. The risk may or may not be worth it to you.

Just be sure your feedback is calm and factual so others trust your words. Name-calling in all caps with multiple exclamation points only makes you look like a hothead, as seen in Figure 1-5. Remember that people tend to read the profiles of *both* people involved in a dispute, so retaliatory feedback is pretty easy to spot (and disregard).

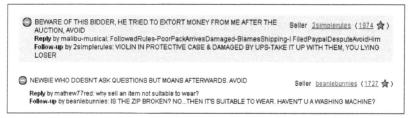

Figure 1-5. How you respond to feedback can be more important than the feedback itself. Who would you believe—the raving lunatic or the person who kept his cool? Stick to the facts and don't make it personal.

Fees, Like a Closed Mind, Can't Be Changed

Leslie bid on a pair of Hello Kitty oven mitts with clearly stated shipping charges of $4.50.

After she won and the seller invoiced her, she noticed the cost for shipping had doubled. When Leslie questioned the seller about it, he told her he made a mistake in the listing and besides, she got such a great deal she had no room to complain.

Leslie wasn't happy but feared being filed against as a *non-paying bidder* if she refused to pay what the seller wanted.

Avoid it!

A seller is never permitted to demand (or even ask for) additional fees. If he does, the buyer should politely but firmly remind him that an auction's terms of service are binding. Just as a buyer can't pay less than a winning bid, a seller can't tack on extra fees after the fact.

There are times when it's wise to exercise some flexibility, of course. If you feel a mistake in a listing was an honest one, you may want to discuss some sort of compromise with the seller. Just don't let him make you feel you have to accept a set of brand-new terms.

Escape it!

If the seller refuses to budge, you can file a report with eBay by going to Help → Report problems with other eBay members → Problems with sellers → Seller asked for additional fees after listing ended.

Should the seller still refuse to accept payment in the proper amount, file a *Non-Performing Seller Report* as well (at Help → A to Z → N → Non-Selling Seller). Keep all emails from the seller, since eBay will want to see them as proof of your claim.

NOTE   Just because a seller files an unpaid item dispute and issues a non-paying strike against you doesn't mean you have to live with it. eBay has a process in place to dispute such things at *http://pages.ebay.com/help/ tp/appeal-upi.html*. If you can prove the seller refused to sell to you under the terms of the auction, eBay will remove the strike and reprimand the seller. And, of course, you can always leave appropriate feedback for him as well.

Pardon Me, Your Shill Is Showing

Daniel found a vintage Grateful Dead concert poster and placed a proxy bid early in the auction.

An hour before it closed, another bidder "nibbled" at Daniel's proxy bit by bit before finally surpassing it. The bidder then retracted her last bid, which left Daniel's bid at its maximum.

The 60s may have been a blur, but he had a nagging feeling everything wasn't on the up and up here.

Avoid it!

Shill bidding or *shilling* is the act of a seller (or an accomplice) using another ID to bid on her own item to drive up the price. It's not permitted on eBay and is even considered a crime in many states.

As a buyer, the best way to avoid being shilled is to bid late in an auction. You should also generally try to avoid *private auctions*, which hide bidder identities and make shilling harder to spot (see Figure 1-6).

private listing - bidders' identities protected	US $8.00	Dec-20-05 19:24:01 PST
private listing - bidders' identities protected	US $7.50	Dec-21-05 21:00:19 PST
private listing - bidders' identities protected	US $6.50	Dec-21-05 21:00:08 PST
private listing - bidders' identities protected	US $5.00	Dec-21-05 08:49:47 PST
private listing - bidders' identities protected	US $1.80	Dec-21-05 08:49:26 PST

Figure 1-6. A private auction's bid history page shows only the bid amounts and when they were placed—not the IDs of the people who placed them. While there are some legitimate uses for private auctions, they're often used to hide shilling activity and should generally be avoided.

As a rule, the only legitimate private auctions are those in the Mature Audiences category. Some extremely exclusive, very expensive items also use the private auction format to protect the bidders from being spammed by other sellers and to prevent fraudulent Second Chance Offers. (See Chapter 6 for more on this.)

So unless you're buying a sex toy or an original Picasso, steer clear of private auctions.

Escape it!

The only thing you can do as a buyer is to stall your payment for a few days while eBay investigates. Report your suspicions of shilling to eBay by going to *http://pages.ebay.com/help/policies/seller-shill-bidding.html* (Figure 1-7). When you get there, click the "report" link at the top. (For more on this, see the following sidebar, "Sherlock the Shillers.")

For privacy reasons, eBay won't usually tell you what they found—but if you get an email from eBay stating the auction was pulled or the seller was NARU'd, you'll know you were right and you won't be on the hook to pay for the auction. (For the uninitiated, NARU stands for *Not a Registered User*.)

WARNING You should never, ever pay a NARU'd seller. Period. Exclamation point. Select your punctuation of choice, but do it while refusing to pay the seller. The seller can't leave feedback for you while he's suspended so you have nothing to fear.

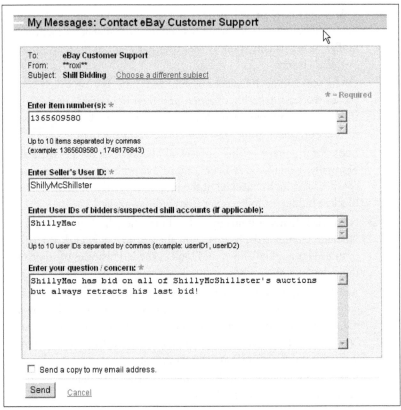

Figure 1-7. The form to report shilling. Make sure you have the usernames of both the seller and the suspected shill, and include why you believe shilling is going on.

Sherlock the Shillers

One of the questions we get most often in the Answer Center is "How can I tell if a seller is shilling?" Ferreting out this type of activity is usually not terribly complicated—most shillers slip up somewhere. Often all it takes is a little sleuthing in the right place to confirm (or dispel) your suspicions.

Start at the Advanced Search page, linked from the upper right of every eBay page.

- First, go to Items → Items by Bidder. Enter the bidder's ID and select "Include Completed Listings" and "Even if not the high bidder." The search results show you the auctions on which the bidder has had an active bid in the past 30 days.

  Has the bidder bid exclusively (or almost exclusively) on only one seller's auctions? Some buyers find a seller they like and stick with her—but has the bidder actually *won* any of that seller's auctions? Shillers don't usually want to win; they just want to push up someone else's proxy.

  Often the shilling ID places several bids, the last of which surpasses the legitimate high bidder, and then the seller cancels only the most recent bid. This leaves the legitimate bidder's proxy maxed out, thus raising the overall price of the auction.

  Look for a pattern of this on several auctions, as it's not typical. Normally, when a seller is uncomfortable with a bidder and cancels her bids, he'll cancel *all* of them and then add the bidder to his blocked bidder list to keep her from bidding again.

- Next, click Items → Items by Seller. Enter the seller's ID and select "Include Completed Listings." On the results page, click the column header marked "End" and look at the bid histories of some of the older, closed auctions.

  Are there any auctions in which the seller canceled all of the suspicious ID's bids? Or auctions where the ID retracted all her own bids? This would prevent the auction from showing up in an "Items by Bidder" search (only auctions with at least one remaining active bid from an ID are shown there).

  While some sellers try to hide shilling activity by doing this, it's not a very effective way to shill so it's less common.

—continued—

- Back at the Advanced Search page, go to Members → Find a Member. Enter the ID of the seller. If the ID is registered in the United States, you'll be able to see what state the person is in. Do a similar search on the suspected shilling ID.

  Are both people in the same state? This is a less precise way of spotting shillers because there are possibly millions of registered eBay users from a particular state, not to mention the fact that it's possible to use bogus information when registering an ID. But checking the state sometimes provides useful information.

- Finally, click the suspicious bidder's feedback number, which takes you to his feedback page. Directly underneath the box labeled "Recent Ratings" is a notation for "Bid Retractions (Past 6 months)."

  How many retractions are noted? One or two retractions aren't necessarily cause for concern, but numerous retractions may indicate an ID used for shilling.

Keep in mind that only eBay staff has the tools that definitively determine shilling activity. Regardless of what your amateur detective work turns up, you should never accuse someone outright of shilling—report your suspicions to eBay and let the staff handle it at an official level.

2

Don't Get Burned on Payment

"A fool and his money are soon parted," or so the saying goes.

But intelligence often has little to do with it. Even a smartypants may find his pockets empty if he zigs when he should zag.

The payment process is like a minefield, and the bombs don't care if you're a buyer or a seller—but if you know where to step, the whole thing is perfectly harmless (which also makes it like the beach where my neighbors walk their dogs). Consider this chapter your map. And wipe your shoes before you come in the house.

PayPal: Read the Fine Print

PayPal is the most common form of payment on eBay. By some estimates, as much as 80 percent of eBay users are registered with the popular payment service. That's a whole lot of money flowing back and forth, and a whole lot of room for error on your part.

PayPal is remarkably safe for both buyers and sellers, but it does have rules that must be followed—for both your protection and that of your trading partner.

Local Pickup Means No Proof of Delivery

Adam listed and sold a laptop computer on eBay. After the auction was over, he received an email from the buyer, who lived in a neighboring town and wanted to pick up the laptop rather than have it shipped.

Since packing and shipping electronics safely can be tricky, Adam was happy to oblige. The buyer issued payment via PayPal and came by Adam's house to get the computer the following day.

About a month later, he received a notice from PayPal stating the buyer claimed non-receipt of the item and wanted his money back. Confused, Adam emailed and called the buyer but didn't get a response.

Since he couldn't prove the buyer received the computer, PayPal forced him to refund the buyer's money.

Avoid it!

If you're the seller, don't use PayPal for items picked up locally—in those situations, you should insist on cash.

One of PayPal's *Seller Protection* rules (see the section "It's Smart to Use Protection" later in this chapter) is you must have proof of delivery that can be tracked online such as a *delivery confirmation* number from the USPS, a tracking number from UPS, etc.—anything that can be accessed online and show the item was actually delivered. For items that sell for $250 or more, the rules are even more stringent in that the package must be signed for upon delivery.

If a buyer files a *complaint of non-receipt,* the first thing PayPal does is ask the seller for a DC or *tracking number.* If you don't have it, PayPal will almost always require you to refund the buyer's money.

Even if you require the buyer to sign a receipt of some kind, you're not protected with PayPal. You *must* have that electronic tracking number.

Escape it!

While a signed receipt won't be worth the paper it's written on to PayPal, it could be worth quite a lot in court. Yes, Perry Mason, I said "in court."

> **N O T E**   Want to see your sneaky thief squirm in front of
> Judge Judy or Judge Marilyn? Televised court shows
> love eBay disputes (I know this because I TiVo those
> shows—shut up). Submit your dispute for consider-
> ation at *http://www.judgejudy.com* or *http://www.*
> *peoplescourt.com.*

Suing someone in small claims court requires a little paperwork and a
small filing fee (typically around $50). You must sue the person in her
jurisdiction—but if the item was picked up locally, chances are good
the buyer lives nearby, so your travel expenses should be minimal.

Best of all, there are no lawyers and no juries in small claims court—
just you, your thieving buyer, and the judge. So all you have to do is
convince the judge you're telling the truth and he'll enter a judg-
ment against the buyer, compelling her to cough up the cash she
essentially stole from you.

And back at eBay, file an *Unpaid Item Dispute* (Figure 2-1).

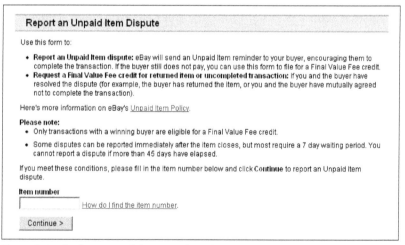

Figure 2-1. The first page of the Unpaid Item Dispute. Here's where you'll enter the
item number of the auction for which you haven't been paid. Curses on deadbeat
bidders!

Revenge of the Sellers

Far too often when a seller isn't paid for whatever reason (see the "My Cat Is a Shopaholic" later in this chapter), she thinks all she can do is relist the item and leave the buyer negative feedback.

Au contraire.

To keep the buyer from stiffing other sellers, it's crucial to file and later close an Unpaid Item Dispute (commonly called a UPI). Unfortunately, a lot of sellers think the process is too complicated to bother—and while I admit it could be a bit more user-friendly, it ain't nuclear science. And it'll put money in your pocket!

Here's how it works: start at My eBay → Dispute Console → Report an Unpaid Item. Exactly seven days (to the minute) after the end of the auction, you can file the UPI. This automatically kicks out an email from eBay to your buyer. The email reminds the buyer to pay for the auction and warns of the consequences if he doesn't.

Now one of a couple things may happen. If the buyer coughs up the money he owes you, you can go into your *Dispute Console* (see Figure 2-2) and close the dispute, stating you've received payment (but make sure you actually *have* the payment before you do that—don't close the dispute on the promise of a payment). You'll ship the item and that'll be the end of it.

But if he ignores you and/or still won't pay, go back to your Dispute Console a week after the UPI was filed and you'll see a checkmark next to the dispute. View the dispute and then close it, selecting as the reason "I no longer wish to wait for or communicate with the buyer."

When you do that, you'll be refunded your *Final Value Fees* (the percentage eBay takes off the final selling price) and given a relist credit—meaning if you relist the item within 90 days and it sells the second time around, eBay will refund that second set of insertion fees (excluding enhancements like gallery photos). You will, of course, be responsible for the final value fees since you were refunded those from the first auction.

Closing the dispute in this manner also assigns the buyer a non-paying bidder strike, and that's what's really important. Any buyer who racks up a bunch of strikes within a certain period of time will have his eBay account suspended.

—continued—

So by following the UPI process to its conclusion, you're not only getting back the money eBay charged you to sell the item, you're helping keep the site clear of deadbeats.

Win-win, wouldn't you say?

NOTE   The email the buyer gets when you file a UPI tells him the item may no longer be available, so you can relist the item as soon as you file—but you'll only get a *listing* credit if you wait to relist until after the dispute is closed. All the rules about relisting are at *http://pages.ebay.com/help/sell/relist.html*.

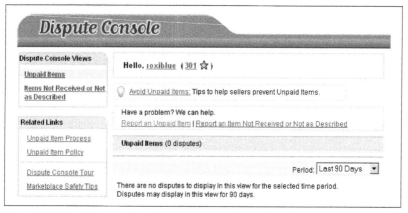

Figure 2-2. Your Dispute Console can be accessed from the left navigation column of your My eBay page.

Confirmed Addresses Are Your Friends

Upon her therapist's recommendation, Pam decided to sell her diamond engagement ring after getting divorced ("closure" and all). The ring received several bids and sold for $1,500.

She accepted a credit card payment through PayPal and shipped the ring with insurance and signature confirmation. According to the USPS web site, the ring was signed for and delivered less than a week later.

Shortly after that, Pam received notification from PayPal that the buyer used a stolen credit card and the payment had therefore been reversed.

Pam scheduled a few more appointments with her therapist to deal with the loss of not only her ring, but also her money.

Avoid it!

As a seller, Pam followed PayPal's rules for shipment by getting signature confirmation for her expensive item but she overlooked another important rule: in order to qualify for Seller Protection, items must be shipped to a confirmed address.

Address confirmation is a PayPal process whereby the buyer submits a credit card and PayPal matches up the card's billing address to the mailing address the buyer submitted when he opened up his PayPal account. If those addresses match, the buyer's account is marked as "confirmed."

It's a security measure because if someone has stolen a credit card (or just a credit card number), he likely won't know the billing address for the card—and even if he does, the address where he'd want the merchandise shipped would almost certainly be different.

So to protect against credit card fraud, PayPal insists sellers ship to confirmed addresses to qualify for PayPal's Seller Protection.

If Pam's buyer had, for example, stolen his roommate's credit card and used it, the billing and shipping addresses would have matched. PayPal would have confirmed his address and even if the roommate later reported the card as stolen, Pam would've been protected—and permitted to keep the money.

Now, while the general lesson here for sellers is to ship to confirmed addresses, I want to qualify that with a dose of common sense.

Some people don't have credit cards or are uncomfortable giving those numbers even to a reputable company like PayPal—and without a credit card number, address confirmation is difficult. But don't automatically assume someone whose address is unconfirmed is a scammer.

Think for a moment about what someone would use a stolen credit card to purchase—high-end electronics, jewelry, designer handbags, etc. In other words, expensive bling. No one's going to commit a crime to gain access to your Aunt Tilly's collection of schnauzer figurines.

So if that dog-loving buyer has an unconfirmed address, it's probably safe to ship to him. But for pricey items, it's best to protect yourself by insisting on a confirmed address.

If you like, you can change your PayPal preferences to require your approval for payments from unconfirmed addresses (see Figure 2-3). That way, you'll at least have an option before accepting payment.

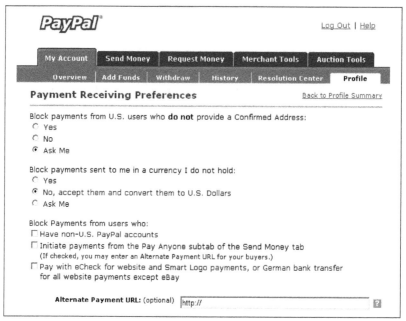

Figure 2-3. Your PayPal preferences allow you to determine how you want to handle payments from people with unconfirmed addresses (among a myriad of other options). Log in to PayPal, click the Profile tab, and then go to Selling Preferences → Payment Receiving Preferences.

Escape it!

Just as in the previous story, court action by the seller is possible but may be more difficult if the buyer lives in a distant state. It's worth a shot to contact the police and possibly even the district attorney in the buyer's jurisdiction, though both may say you need to file any relevant reports in person.

For more advice, go to Help → A to Z → F → Fraud: Information for Sellers.

When It's Okay to Be Xenophobic

Cali listed a sweater (Figure 2-4) and in the auction stated she would ship worldwide. Her winning buyer was from Germany and paid using PayPal.

Figure 2-4. Would you bid on this sweater?

A few weeks later, the buyer filed a non-receipt complaint with PayPal. Cali discovered the buyer was now selling on eBay the very sweater he claimed he never got. She showed the auction to PayPal but her buyer claimed it was a different sweater.

It really didn't matter much anyway—the purchase didn't qualify for PayPal's Seller Protection because Cali failed to get proof of delivery that could be accessed online, and since foreign addresses can rarely be confirmed, she also didn't ship to a confirmed address.

Avoid it!

One of PayPal's more glaring flaws is that it provides very little protection to U.S. sellers who ship internationally.

Until recently, PayPal's *Seller Protection Policy* almost never covered transactions with foreign buyers because foreign addresses couldn't be confirmed. This left sellers wide open to all kinds of fraud. Some rather evil buyers made it a point to purchase from U.S. sellers who accepted PayPal and then routinely claimed those items never arrived.

In May of 2005, PayPal announced it was expanding the methods used for confirming addresses in the U.S., UK, and Canada. This means the Seller Protection Policy (SPP) may cover transactions between buyers and sellers in those countries.

While this is happy news, it doesn't address one other very important SPP requirement: proof of delivery that can be tracked online. It's sometimes possible to purchase it when shipping internationally, but it can be prohibitively expensive and may cost more than the actual postage itself.

Understandably, buyers don't want to pay this extra cost, so unless the seller is willing to pay for it out of her own pocket (which may leave her with no profit from the auction sale), she's right back where she started—if she accepts PayPal for an international transaction, the SPP won't cover her.

PayPal is aware of this Catch-22 and is considering what can be done about it.

One possibility is to require only proof of postage (rather than proof of delivery) for international transactions, but that opens up the possibility for some sellers to exploit the system by purchasing postage for an item they never send. And since a postage receipt can be easily dummied up on any computer, it would be difficult for PayPal to know whom to trust.

Remember old episodes of classic sitcoms where a wall would spring a leak and as soon as someone stuck their finger in the hole to plug it, another leak sprang forth? Yeah, it's kinda like that.

In any case, just as it's advisable to consider the likelihood of fraud when shipping to unconfirmed addresses within the U.S., the same should be done for any international transactions.

Many sellers who ship worldwide will tell you the extra business they get makes the gamble a good one, and fraudulent transactions are such a tiny percentage of their overall sales that it makes good financial sense to take the risk.

NOTE   You can avoid the problem altogether by requiring money order payments from your international customers, but keep in mind many of them won't bid on auctions unless they can pay via PayPal.

Escape it!

Not much you can do as the seller unless you're willing to hop an international flight with a baseball bat.

And I really wouldn't advise that.

Money Order Mayhem and Chaos with Cashier's Checks

A long time ago, in a galaxy far far away, electronic payment methods didn't even exist.

It's Smart to Use Protection

PayPal is quick and convenient, but let's face it, most of its protections are for buyers.

Sellers have a set of protection policies, but certain criteria must be met to take advantage of them. Although some people try to make the rules more complicated than they are, they're actually pretty straightforward.

The full list can be found at *http://www.paypal.com/cgi-bin/webscr?cmd=p/gen/ua/policy_spp-outside*, but here's the fine print boiled down to the important stuff:

- You must ship a tangible item within seven days of payment. Items sent electronically (e-books, for example) aren't covered under the Seller Protection Policy.
- You must ship with an online-trackable form of delivery confirmation.
- If a buyer purchases multiple items and you'll be shipping them in one box, you must accept only one lump-sum payment for everything. Since proof of delivery is required for each transaction processed individually, items paid for separately but mailed together are subject to fraudulent claims of non-receipt.
- Items that sell for $250 or more must be signed for upon delivery.
- You must ship only to the address the buyer has registered with PayPal; for fullest protection, ship only to a confirmed address.
- If you have a dispute filed against you, you must respond to PayPal promptly—usually within seven days, but sometimes in as little as three days.

When to roll the dice:

Although PayPal insists on strict adherence to these rules in order for sellers to qualify for protection, those sellers who stringently follow the rules on even the smallest purchases will cost themselves business.

There are times when it's okay to loosen up a little.

If a buyer has a long history on eBay with lots of great feedback and if a check of the feedback she's left for others doesn't reveal her to be a scammer, it's often all right to send an item to an unconfirmed address—or even to ship to a completely different address if the item is being sent as a gift.

Use some common sense and the vast majority of the time your transactions will be successful.

Hard to believe, I know, but the bouncing baby PayPal wasn't born unto the Mother Internet until October 22, 1999 (right on the cusp of Libra and Scorpio—sexy!). By then, eBay had already been around for four years.

So how were people paying for their used clothing and Pez dispensers?

Unless they wanted to wait for personal checks to clear (we'll get into those later), they sent money orders or cashier's checks. Even today some sellers choose to forego PayPal's convenience factor because of its rules (and fees) and they accept payment only the old-fashioned way.

Money orders and cashier's checks are the same as cash, right? So what could possibly go wrong?

Plenty.

Take the Money Order and Run

Bernie won an auction for a 60-gig iPod from a new eBay seller. The seller stated she hadn't had the time yet to open a PayPal account and could only accept money orders, so Bernie purchased a money order and mailed it to her.

Over the next month he watched in horror as her feedback rating nose-dived and her eBay account was finally suspended. After emailing several of her other recent buyers, he found out he wasn't the only one whose money she stole—well over a dozen other people never received their expensive merchandise either.

Later on it was discovered the P.O. box the seller used was rented in a fictitious name and she cashed the money orders (made out to that alias) at several neighborhood check-cashing outlets using fake ID.

The seller currently has a warrant out for her arrest, but to date she hasn't been found.

Avoid it!

Sellers aren't the only ones who can get burned around here, you know.

As a buyer, you may want to consider purchasing items on eBay only from established sellers. While all eBay sellers have to start somewhere, few do it by selling expensive items right out of the gate. It doesn't necessarily mean they're up to no good, but it does mean you should be cautious.

The plusses of buying from a new seller include the fact that you probably won't have as much competition as you would if you were buying from a more experienced seller—but there's a good reason for that. Savvy bidders who steer clear of such sellers may know something you don't.

If you must ignore their wisdom, at least make sure your unproven seller can accept PayPal—and make sure you pay using a credit card. That way if something goes awry and for whatever reason PayPal can't recover your money, you'll have the added protection of your own credit card company to back you up.

And really, no matter how seasoned your seller may be, you should never pay for an expensive item with a money order. They offer almost no protection to buyers.

Escape it!

The parameters for U.S. mail fraud are much broader than you might think. If you were scammed and sent your payment through the mail, read all about mail fraud (and file a grievance) at *http://www.usps.com/postalinspectors/welcome.htm*. Click the "Mail Fraud" link on the left to bring up the page shown in Figure 2-5.

As for your woefully empty pockets, eBay's *Standard Purchase Protection Program* just may be able to ease your pain, at least in part. Essentially, it's a $200 insurance policy with a $25 deductible.

U.S. Postal Inspection Service

Mail Fraud

Mail Fraud Schemes	U.S. Postal Inspectors investigate any crime in which the U.S. Mail is used to further a scheme--whether it originated in the mail, by telephone, or on the Internet. The use of the U.S.
How to Get Off Mailing Lists	Mail is what makes it mail fraud.
Junk E-Mail (Spam)	If evidence of a postal violation exists, Postal Inspectors may seek prosecutive or administrative action against the violator. However, if money is lost through a fraudulent scheme conducted via the mail, Inspectors lack the authority to ensure you receive a refund
Didn't Get What You Ordered?	and can't require that products, services, or advertisements--on the Internet or elsewhere--be altered.
File a Mail Fraud Complaint	Postal Inspectors base investigations of mail fraud on the number, pattern, and substance of complaints received from the public. The Postal Inspection Service will carefully review the information you provide. We may share the information with other agencies when there is a
Our Privacy Policy	possible violation within their jurisdiction.
Contact Us	If you feel you've been victimized in a fraud scheme that involves the U.S. Mail, submit a Mail Fraud Complaint Form to the U.S. Postal Inspection Service.

I Inspection Service Home I

Figure 2-5. If you didn't get something you paid for, file a USPS mail fraud complaint at http://www.usps.com/postalinspectors/fraud/.

There are a slew of qualifying terms and conditions (read about them at Help → A to Z → P → Purchase Protection Programs) and as I stated above, the coverage is rather limited.

But as my mother says, it's better than a poke in the eye with a sharp stick.

Fake Checks (Imitation Compensation)

Jack sold an expensive digital camera to an overseas buyer and accepted a cashier's check for payment. He deposited the check the same day he mailed the camera and thought nothing more of it.

A week later, his bank called to notify him the cashier's check was counterfeit.

Despite filing charges with local law enforcement and learning the buyer has done this many times (under many eBay IDs), Jack has been unable to prosecute since the buyer lives in a country with which the U.S. has no extradition treaty.

Avoid it!

I saved this story for last because it encompasses much of what we've already discussed and adds a new twist—counterfeiting.

As a seller, you can avoid Jack's situation by waiting to ship your item until you're certain the funds are in your account. Cashier's checks used to be considered as good as cash. After all, you had to purchase them at a bank and a bank would never issue one without having the cash in hand.

Ah, but kids and their pesky computers have changed the world.

Printers and software are now so sophisticated they can easily make very convincing-looking cashier's checks. Often, they'll even have the name of a major bank such as Chase or Bank of America printed right on them. (You can see scans of some phonies at *http://www. bustedupcowgirl.com*, Figure 2-6.)

Figure 2-6. Bustedupcowgirl.com has all kinds of fun with scammers who think they've found a willing victim.

The same is true of money orders. Even a few phony USPS money orders have been found floating around in recent months.

Because of this, it's becoming more and more common for sellers to treat cashier's checks and money orders just as they treat personal checks; i.e., deposit them and wait 10 days to be sure they clear before any merchandise is shipped.

If you don't want to do that, you can always call the issuing bank and they'll be able to tell you if the payment is authentic or not.

WARNING	Don't be snookered just because you see a big, well-known bank's name—it takes no more time to print "Citibank" than it does "Joe's Bank of Commerce." But it's nice to see Joe doing so well for himself. In high school we never thought he'd amount to anything.

Alternatively, accept only USPS Postal Money Orders. While they can also be counterfeited, you can cash them at any post office so you'll immediately know if they're good or not—*before* you ship.

Escape it!

Well, we've already used baseball bats to exact vengeance. You could always mix it up and go with a lead pipe this time. You don't want to be too predictable.

Better yet, skip the physical violence altogether (it's terribly messy) and file a complaint with the Internet Crime Complaint Center at *http://www.ic3.gov*.

Or you can just turn the whole mess into a fun and exciting game of "Clue."

It was Professor Plum in the library with a candlestick. I'm sure of it.

Personal Checks, Cash, and Others

But wait, there's more!

These situations aren't nearly as common but they're worth a mention.

Lost Stash of Cash

Patricia won an auction and told the seller she'd be mailing her payment of $19.77. But rather than sending the standard check or money order, she carefully concealed a $20 bill and sent it via *Registered Mail*.

The seller signed for the envelope but claimed it arrived empty. Patricia complained to eBay but was told that although she could prove the seller received the envelope, she couldn't prove it actually contained the cash.

Avoid it!

I don't really have to tell you not to send cash through the mail, do I?

Even if it isn't pilfered en route, you'll have absolutely no proof the seller received the money. So don't do it.

Escape it!

Unless you want the seller to file against you as a non-paying bidder, you'll have to submit payment again—this time using a much more secure method.

Has That Check Really Cleared?

Carson sold a car to a buyer who wanted to pay with a personal check. Carson explained the check would have to clear before he'd release the car and she agreed. A few days later Carson called his bank and a teller told him the check cleared. He then met with his buyer, signed over the title, gave her the keys, and she drove off.

Two weeks afterwards, Carson's bank informed him the check was stolen and never actually cleared. The bank manager explained that as a courtesy, the bank credited him with the payment prior to clearance because he'd never deposited a bad check before. The teller who told him the check was good just saw the credit for the check in his account and assumed clearance.

Carson couldn't report the car as stolen because he'd already signed over the title, and the only contact information he had for the buyer was a now-defunct email address and a disconnected phone number.

A lawyer advised him to sue the bank.

Avoid it!

Remember the harassment and derision Bill Clinton endured after answering a question with "it depends on what your definition of 'is' is"?

His statement may not be as absurd as you think.

Banks will often credit a good customer with the funds from a check before it actually clears. So before shipping or handing over merchandise (especially pricey merchandise), you'd be wise to ask what your bank's definition of "cleared" is.

And really, if you're selling a car, you should accept only cash on delivery or payment via a bank-to-bank wire transfer (check with your bank about any fees they may charge for this). You can also accompany the buyer to his bank to have a cashier's check drawn up.

Escape it!

There's an old saying: "Everybody hates lawyers until they need one."

If you're the buyer in this situation, a lawyer is your only way out. So say a few mea culpas for the lawyer jokes you told at that cocktail party, find an attorney, and be very, very nice to her.

Wired and Mired

Phoebe won an auction for an expensive massage table from a seller who asked for payment via Western Union wire transfer. The seller asked that the money be wired to a WU near his home in Nashville.

Phoebe lived in Memphis and although she had some qualms about wiring money for an auction payment, she had the seller's home address and thought if there was a problem, he was only a few hours away so finding him wouldn't be difficult.

When she still hadn't received shipment of her table a month later, she learned the seller's name and address were phony and her money had been picked up at a WU location in New Jersey.

Avoid it!

I warned you about this once already but it bears repeating: if you're the buyer, never under any circumstances wire money to a stranger for an auction payment. Western Union has offices worldwide and all someone needs to get his hands on the cash is a control number or "test question." ID may not be required, and the money can be picked up at any of 100,000+ locations anywhere on the planet. Wired money is untraceable and unrecoverable: once it's gone, it's gone.

eBay specifically recommends against using Western Union wire transfers for auction payments (see Help → A to Z → W → Wire Transfers), and you can read WU's page about consumer fraud protection at *http://www.westernunion.com/info/faqSecurity.asp* (Figure 2-7).

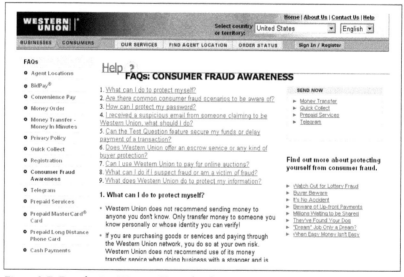

Figure 2-7. Fraud using Western Union has become so common there's a special page on the WU site to warn you about it.

Escape it!

No escaping this one.

It was Miss Scarlet! In the conservatory! With a revolver!

My Cat Is a Shopaholic

The eBay Community forums are full of complaints from sellers whose buyers simply won't pay them.

Non-paying bidders normally reward invoices and other requests for payment with stony silence, but every now and then they'll try to weasel out of paying with a hilariously ridiculous excuse.

I promise you, I didn't make these up.

- "My house burned down and your money order was in it!"
- "I never bid on your item—my cat stepped on the computer mouse while I was in the bathroom."
- "I couldn't have bid—I was in a coma." (A check of the buyer's recent bidding activity showed she bought an awful lot of stuff while supposedly unconscious.)
- "My toddler was clicking around and accidentally bid." (Said child had very discriminating taste—he bid on four BMWs in the same week.)
- "I'm going to some garage sales today. If I have any money left, I'll pay you."
- "I bought this wedding dress for my sister, and her fiancé was an FBI agent killed in a shoot out last week so there won't be a wedding." (The buyer continued to bid on wedding items for weeks afterwards.)
- "I did a Tarot card reading on you and it said you're going to die, so I'm afraid if I pay you you'll die before you send my stuff."

—continued—

- "I was drunk when I bid. If I can't remember it, it doesn't count." (Oh, if only that underlying principle were true.)
- "Your last name sounds foreign. I won't send money to terrorists."
- "I work for NASA and was just informed I'll be going into space."
- "I bid on two of the same thing and God told me to pay for the other one."
- "The tattoo I just got was more expensive than I thought it would be."
- "I was called into service to put down a rebel uprising."
- "I am a Christian and was bidding behind my husband's back. I can be a better witness for Jesus if I back out of my bids."
- "I changed my medication, so I forgot about the auction."

3

Don't Get Burned on Packaging

Let's say you had a smooth-as-silk transaction with a friendly seller who shipped promptly (with a *tracking number*, of course), so now all you have to do is sit back and await the arrival of your fabulous Tiffany lamp.

One glorious morning, a handsome delivery man (or a gorgeous delivery woman—your choice) arrives with your eagerly awaited package. You sign for it, take it inside, and joyfully rip open the box only to find a disaster.

The seller wrapped your delicate lampshade in flimsy brown paper before tossing it into the box. Those colorful glass shards will sure come in handy if you ever find a mosaic art project, but you had something a little more *intact* in mind.

Or perhaps your newly acquired Aeron chair is missing its wheels because the old, battered box in which it was packed tore in transit, resulting in the loss of the small pieces.

Now what?

If you're the buyer in a situation where your auction item has arrived in bad shape, you should start by contacting the seller. If you aren't satisfied with the resolution the seller proposes, you can file an INR/ SNAD complaint with eBay by going to Help → A to Z → I → Item Not Received/Significantly Not As Described Process (Figure 3-1). You can also file a grievance with PayPal, providing you used it for payment (see Chapter 2, "PayPal: Read the Fine Print").

Report an Item Not Received

It's rare for a transaction to go wrong on eBay, but sometimes problems can occur. If you've got a problem with a transaction the Item Not Received or Significantly Not as Described Process can help you resolve it.

Use this process when:
- You paid for an item but didn't receive it, or
- You paid for and received an item, but it was significantly different from the item description.

The most effective way to resolve transaction problems is direct and open communication between buyers and sellers. Once you initiate this process you will be able to communicate directly with your seller on the eBay Web site in order to resolve your problem.

Before you initiate this process, please make sure you have:
- Reviewed the item listing carefully.
- Emailed and called your seller.
- Ensured eBay has your correct contact information.
- Checked your spam filter for missed emails.

Learn more about the steps you should take before initiating this process.

You can begin this process at any time between 10 days and 60 days after the listing ended. Please enter the item number below and click **Continue** to get started.

Item number

How do I find the item number?

Continue >

Note: Information gathered in this process will be stored by eBay for risk management purposes and will be accessible by both parties and eBay.

Figure 3-1. The first page of the INR/SNAD report. After entering the item number, you'll provide relevant details—and if you paid with PayPal, you'll be automatically directed there to file a grievance as well.

If you're an eBay seller, this chapter is primarily for you. You'll learn that a little conscientious care and a bit of common sense are usually all it takes to keep your items safe and your buyers happy.

Don't Use Inadequate Packaging

Bad packing is a big cause of grief between buyers and sellers: the seller feels his packing job was just fine but the buyer has a damaged item to prove otherwise.

Even the most securely packaged items can break in transit, but that doesn't mean you get to be sloppy and blame it on the shipping company. As a seller, you're responsible for getting items to your buyer in the condition in which they were purchased, so unless you enjoy issuing refunds, you'd better pack things well.

NOTE   Items that arrive broken are considered "signifi-cantly not as described" unless the auction stated the item was already broken. PayPal used to stay out of so-called "quality" issues but will now often inter-vene if the buyer can provide photographs or other proof of damage. See Chapter 4 for more details.

Box Size Matters

Joyce sold a lovely Waterford crystal vase. She wrapped it in bubble wrap and found a box sturdy enough to survive the trip to her buyer's home a few states away.

Getting the wrapped vase into the box wasn't easy. The bubble wrap added a couple of inches to the width, so Joyce had to wedge the vase in. It made the sides of the box bulge a bit but she was certain the bubble wrap would provide all the protection necessary.

A week later, her buyer emailed to say the vase did indeed arrive in one piece but was cracked in several places. After receiving proof of the damage, Joyce sadly refunded her buyer's money.

Avoid it!

Selecting the appropriate box for a fragile item is extremely impor-tant. You want to make sure the box isn't big enough for the item to rattle around but not so small that the sides of the box are pushing in on the item.

Many eBay sellers who routinely ship delicate items recommend double-boxing them. This means placing the item in a box with appropriate padding (such as bubble wrap) and then placing that box in a larger box. The second box should be at least 2" bigger than the first on all sides, and that extra space should be loosely filled with packing peanuts.

N O T E   Wadded up newspaper is a poor choice for package
           padding. It can easily compress during shipment and
           leave your item unprotected.

Double-boxing ensures that even if the sides of the outer box are compressed, the interior box (and the item itself) remains intact.

Keep in mind a box is often stacked under other boxes while in shipment. Your package should be able to withstand considerable weight without putting pressure on the delicate item inside, but there can't be so much room around your item that the box collapses in on itself. (A box rated at 200 lbs per square inch is good and durable.)

Yes, it's more expensive to use two boxes instead of one, but it saves you money in the long run since you won't have to issue refunds for items broken in transit. Additionally, if you insure your items, the chance of getting a refund from the carrier increases since you packaged so well.

N O T E   Act as though you're packing items for a move cross-
           country. Good shipping boxes are typically the same
           weight as moving boxes and should be packed in
           much the same way. See *http://discountbox.com/mv_
           dsh.htm* for several quick but thorough tutorials in
           how to best pack items like dishes, crystal, figurines,
           and electronics.

Escape it!

As Joyce (the seller in our story) learned, inadequate packaging can wind up being very expensive—sometimes more expensive than the proper packing materials. If you're in her situation, follow her lead: request proof of the damage and refund your buyer.

Now, if you're a buyer who receives a damaged item, the first thing to do is contact your seller. Be prepared to provide photographic evidence of the damage if and when you're asked for it.

If the item is insured, the seller may ask you to cooperate in an insurance claim. This involves allowing the shipping company to inspect the packaging (it's *imperative* that you keep the box, packing materials, etc.) and/or filling out any necessary forms. Returning the item to the seller before going through this process voids the insurance, so *don't* send it back unless you're specifically asked to do so.

NOTE	If you receive a package and notice significant damage to the box or you can tell from—gently!—shaking it that something inside is broken, grab a camera. Take pictures of the unopened box and/or the damaged item (if the damage is apparent when you open the box, don't remove the item from the packaging to take the photo). You want the photo to show how everything looked when it arrived.

Bubble Wrap Ain't Bulletproof

Marc bid on and won two ceramic coffee mugs emblazoned with the name of his favorite sports team. When they arrived, they were in a bubble envelope and one mug was completely smashed to bits.

The seller said since Marc didn't purchase insurance, she couldn't help him. She wrote FRAGILE all over the envelope and everything! So it wasn't *her* fault the Post Office broke the mug.

Avoid it!

If you're a seller, always, always, *always* pack breakables in a firm, sturdy box.

Some people seem to believe the mere existence of bubble wrap keeps things intact, as though the little air-filled pockets are some kind of magical force field. But no amount of bubble wrap will protect a fragile item in an otherwise flimsy paper envelope. Even packages that say "fragile" are routinely tossed around and wind up with heavy items on top of them.

And, by the way, even if someone had purchased insurance for the package in our story, any claim with the carrier would have been denied because one of the conditions of any insurance payout is that the item must be well packed.

Escape it!

As the seller, you don't have to take the buyer's word for it that something has arrived broken. Ask to see pictures of the damage.

You can then decide whether to refund his money outright or ask for the item to be returned to you first. Just be careful if the item is insured. As I said above, returning an insured item without going through the claims process voids the insurance.

If you ask for the item's return, you're not required to pay for return shipping, but you really should anyway. It's not the buyer's fault his mug arrived broken and while it may not be yours either, it's good customer service to make your buyer "whole" by refunding every penny he paid (or replacing the item with an exact duplicate, if possible). Your feedback will reflect your generosity (or lack thereof).

If you decide to ask for the item's return, don't refund a dime until you have it back. If you issue a refund first, you'll have little recourse should the buyer "forget" to return the package to you.

Insurance claims should be completed before you refund money as well. (See Figure 3-2 for filing insurance claims with USPS.) By that I mean the buyer has cooperated fully in the process and you're simply awaiting a decision from the carrier.

Refund the buyer's money after the forms have been submitted and the item checked by the carrier because if the claim is approved, you'll receive reimbursement yourself from the shipping company. If your claim is denied, it's likely your packaging was substandard (which is your fault and not the buyer's so he should still get his money back).

Figure 3-2. You can access USPS insurance guidelines, rules and forms at http://www.usps.com/insuranceclaims/welcome.htm.

WARNING   Some buyers are less than honest. I'm sure you're clutching your pearls in open-mouthed horror but it's true. I discuss some increasingly common buyer scams in Chapter 6.

Paper Isn't Much Better

Brianne purchased a pair of Donna Karan pants from an eBay seller.

When she received them, she saw the manila envelope in which they were mailed was torn. The Post Office wrapped the package in cellophane during transit to ensure the pants actually got to her, but they had apparently fallen out at some point and were dirty and stained.

The seller claimed he'd never had a problem sending items in paper envelopes before, and using them instead of boxes helped keep his shipping costs low.

Avoid it!

If you're the seller, don't choose plain manila envelopes for mailing soft or bulky items. As anyone over the age of conception knows, paper tears.

Packages often come in contact with machines and conveyer belts that can easily rip a hole in an envelope. If that happens, the item may fall to the floor in the shipping facility. If you're lucky, someone will spot it when it happens, match it up with its envelope and the item will arrive at its intended destination (albeit the worse for wear).

If you're not so lucky, the item will be completely lost and the buyer will receive an empty envelope with a note from the carrier stating the packaging was insufficient and resulted in the loss of the item. Neither situation is a good one, so ship in something more substantial.

The seller in the above example is correct about one thing—paper is lighter than cardboard, so the postage usually costs less than that of a box. That, however, isn't a valid reason to ship something irresponsibly. It doesn't do much good to save a couple of dollars on shipping if you wind up having to refund the entire purchase price because the item is lost or damaged.

There's good news. Something lightweight *and* sturdy does exist, and I use it all the time. It's called Tyvek. You've probably received items in Tyvek envelopes before, even if you didn't know exactly what the material was called. It resembles fiberglass and is what many FedEx and USPS envelopes are made of.

Tyvek is incredibly strong stuff (in fact, some bulletproof vests are constructed from it)—tear-resistant, water-resistant, puncture-resistant, and even recyclable. It's also light as a feather, making it the perfect choice for shipping items like clothing, towels, and bedding. Just about anything soft and/or unbreakable travels nicely in Tyvek. It's probably my favorite way to ship things.

You can get the envelopes at many office supply stores and online retail sites (or do an eBay search for "Tyvek envelopes" to find sellers who have them). The envelopes come in a bunch of sizes, so finding one that suits your needs won't be difficult.

Escape it!

If you're the seller, there's no escaping this one. Pay the lady!

If you're the buyer, photograph the evidence (or lack thereof) and alert the seller, letting him know you expect a refund. Be polite but firm.

NOTE   If you're going to use USPS Priority, Express, or Global Mail shipping, you can get Tyvek envelopes for free at the post office or by visiting *http://shop.usps.com*. But keep in mind you can't simply turn the envelopes inside out and use them any way you like. That's considered mail fraud and the USPS isn't shy about calling you on it.

"Do Not Bend" Does Not Work

Sheila won an auction for a vintage clothing catalog.

Her apartment mailbox is tall and narrow, so she asked the seller to be certain the catalog was packaged in such a manner that it couldn't be folded (and thus, damaged).

She was dismayed when her item arrived—folded lengthwise and stuffed in her mailbox. The only precaution the seller had taken was to write DO NOT BEND on the envelope, which was either overlooked or ignored by Sheila's postal carrier.

Avoid it!

As a seller, you should know there are really only two acceptable ways to ship ephemera (the fancy word for "collectible paper items" like catalogs, comic books, etc.).

The first is in a box, since boxes can't be folded in half and stuffed into mail receptacles.

The second is in an envelope, but it must have some kind of hard backing that can't be folded. Corrugated cardboard usually works nicely. Sandwich the item between two pieces of cardboard and you should be good to go. Be sure the cardboard is larger than the item it's protecting. Corners get bumped and bent in travel, and you want the cardboard taking the brunt of it.

Also, wrap the item in some kind of plastic before it goes into the envelope. That way, if the envelope gets wet and soaks the cardboard, it won't ruin the item inside.

It's never a bad idea to write DO NOT BEND on the envelope, but package the item under the assumption that it may get bent anyway. All these precautions should be taken no matter how "collectible" the item actually is. You don't know why the buyer purchased it (it could be for sentimental reasons or a gift) and regardless, they'll want it to arrive undamaged.

Escape it!

If you're buying ephemera, ask the seller about her packaging before you bid. If rigid backing isn't mentioned, request it—and don't bid unless she agrees. Keep the correspondence until your item arrives. If it's damaged due to negligent packaging, you'll have proof you specifically asked for the item to be packed differently.

Don't Use Odd or Potentially Embarrassing Packaging

This is less important than ensuring an item arrives undamaged, but it's a close second.

If you pack your items in a way that removes the allure of what your buyers purchase or worse yet, causes them to become red-faced in front of delivery people, exactly how eager do you think they'll be to buy from you again?

Right. So if you want glowing feedback and repeat business, pay attention to detail. Your buyers will thank you for it.

Box Bonanza

Okay, so I've hammered into your head the importance of sufficient packaging and now you're wondering—where can I get good packing materials without spending all the profits from my sales?

I thought you'd never ask.

If you're new to eBay, one of the best ways to build up your feedback (see the "Don't Be Quick on the Feedback Trigger" section in Chapter 5) in anticipation of becoming a seller is to buy some shipping supplies from other eBay sellers.

A couple of shipping supply companies I can recommend (though this certainly isn't an exhaustive list) are gatorpack at *http://stores.ebay.com/ Gatorpack-Shipping-Supplies* and parrothead88 at *http://stores.ebay.com/ Shipping-Supplies-CHEAP*. I have personal experience with both of them. They do a tremendous volume of business yet they also have great customer service, fair shipping rates, and unbelievably good feedback. Of course, you can always browse for a seller on your own, too—go to Buy → Business & Industrial → Office Printing & Shipping → Shipping & Packing Supplies (see Figure 3-3).

Figure 3-3. Within the Shipping & Packing Supplies category, you'll find everything from bubble mailers to boxes. Buying in bulk usually saves you money, but watch the shipping fees and be sure to factor them in to determine your final per-piece cost.

—continued—

If you're already an eBay seller and feel that even the cheapest supplies are breaking the bank, you may be able to score them for free—if you know where to look. Here's one of the better-kept secrets: find a local gift shop that routinely sells fragile collectibles like porcelain figurines, decorative plates, crystal bells, etc. Speak to the store owner or manager and ask what she does with the boxes, bubble wrap, and packing peanuts she gets when she receives a shipment of items.

If she says she throws them away or recycles them, you've struck gold. Tell her you'd love to take the mess off her hands and ask how often you should come by. Most stores receive their merchandise on the same day each week or month, so you should be prepared to arrange your own schedule around theirs.

Be sure you know exactly how much you'll be expected to haul away. Some store owners insist on an "all or nothing" deal. If the "all" is manageable for you, terrific—but check first to see if it'll be a box of packing peanuts or a truckful. Lots of merchants are happy to give you their supplies because trash and recycling services are expensive. Usually the more that's tossed, the more it costs.

Furniture stores are good sources for packing material. They often get lamps and side tables wrapped in bubble wrap or shipped in boxes with packing peanuts. If they're not shipping items, they may be happy to have you haul away the "trash."

If you just need boxes, there's at least one old stand-by: grocery stores. Just make sure the boxes you pilfer are clean and dry. Buyers don't want items packed in slimy cardboard. They're funny that way.

You can also get free boxes from many shipping companies, as long as you're willing to ship via that particular carrier. See the note in the "Paper Isn't Much Better" section earlier in this chapter for USPS supplies, and visit *http://www.ups.com* and *http://www.fedex.com* to order supplies from UPS and FedEx, respectively.

Finally, there's something you can do to kill two birds with one proverbial stone. Shop online. A lot. And save the shipping supplies and boxes other people use to send items to you. It may not be the least expensive way to get what you need, but it's certainly the most fun.

What You Buy Is No One Else's Business

Jody recently had a baby, and despite her best efforts she couldn't seem to get back to her pre-pregnancy weight. Her friends had been raving about a particular diet supplement called Poundz Aweigh, so Jody found an authorized seller of the product on eBay and ordered a three-month supply.

When her package arrived, she was horrified to see the box was brightly emblazoned with the company's slogan: "Poundz Aweigh! Winning the War Against Fat!" Making matters worse, the delivery driver left the package on Jody's doorstep while she was at work, so all her neighbors saw it.

That evening she was treated to a lecture from the doctor next door who told her supplements don't work, and the New Age-y couple across the street called to say she should accept herself and be at peace with who she is.

Avoid it!

Sellers of adult-oriented items have long been advocates of the "plain brown envelope," and for good reason: what's in the package is no one's business. Even if it isn't something the kids shouldn't see, that doesn't mean the buyer's right to privacy should be disregarded.

If you're selling items on behalf of a company and that entity insists on putting its logo on the outside of the shipping box, you should warn potential buyers about this in your auction. That way they'll at least know what to expect.

And it's perfectly fine to reuse packaging (like those grocery store boxes you scored) but if the ideal box for your item is stamped with the name of a well-known laxative, at least use a heavy black marker to make it unrecognizable. You can also cover the offending words with opaque tape or wrap the entire box with brown paper.

Putting aside the embarrassment factor for a moment, keep in mind it's possible your buyer is purchasing an item as a gift. So when you ship a box proclaiming its contents, you're alerting everyone in the buyer's family that Timmy is finally getting the radio-controlled helicopter he's been wanting.

Way to ruin an eight-year-old's birthday! I'll bet you kick puppies for fun, too.

Escape it!

If something you're buying will be a gift for a member of your household, be sure to let the seller know and ask him to obscure any indication of what's inside the box. The same is true if you're buying something you'd rather the neighbors not snicker about every time they see you.

Looks Matter—Even with Packages

Sandra was a big fan of a particular European bra. It fit her perfectly but retailed for more than $65 (a lot of money for Sandra). While browsing eBay one day, she was thrilled to find the bra in a color she didn't yet have. She placed a bid and won the auction, getting a good price on the bra.

A couple of weeks later, she received a small box wrapped in brown paper. Her fabulous new bra had arrived! She happily tore off the outside paper to reveal... a frozen enchilada box (Figure 3-4). Her exotic French unmentionable was wrapped in a plastic bag so it was clean, but that box sure put a dent in her enthusiasm.

The seller had other bras Sandra would have considered purchasing, but she chose to spend a little more and buy from a seller who wrapped her items in pretty tissue paper and mailed them in plain bubble mailers instead.

Avoid it!

Presentation is an important and often overlooked part of selling.

Figure 3-4. The scene of the crime. When's the last time you got to see a girl's undies without buying her dinner first? Bow in gratitude, peasant!

If you think the story above is absurd, think again. It happened to me, exactly as I described it. And yes, I found another seller. I was actually willing to spend more money on the exact same item in the exact same condition—simply because of the way I felt when I opened the package.

Tiffany and Co. is one of the world's most renowned brands largely because it understands the importance of good presentation. The company is almost as famous for its robin's-egg-blue boxes as for the elegant jewelry inside. This doesn't mean you need your own specialty packaging, but you can still learn a lesson from Tiffany's: chic, simple presentation enhances an item and makes your customer feel special.

Even the most mundane items can benefit from good presentation. One clothing seller I know wraps everything she sells in tissue and then ties the parcel in ribbon before it goes into the box. The end result is that even a plain T-shirt looks striking when the package is opened.

One of my favorite eBay sellers, colorful*sprinkles, tosses a handful of small, brightly colored foam cutouts in various shapes into her packages. They look like, well, colorful sprinkles. She's not only enhancing her presentation, she's reinforcing her brand name.

WARNING   Don't include anything that may be a safety hazard. You may think a piece of hard candy would be a fun touch—but your buyer with the diabetic child (and sugar-free household) probably won't be very happy about it. And don't include anything that requires a buyer to vacuum or sweep after your package is opened. A fistful of glitter may look pretty, but it'll make a mess.

It's equally important that your package not emit odors when opened. If you smoke, keep the items you're selling and your packaging materials far away from the smoke since packaging tends to soak up the smell. And if your home has central heat or air, you're better off smoking outside. Air ducts pull smoke through the house into other rooms.

On the flip side, some sellers think it's a nice touch to add something that smells *good* to a package, like dryer sheets or those paper fragrance samples pulled from magazines, but that's really not such a spiffy idea either. Your buyer (or one of her family members) may have allergies or chemical sensitivities, and you don't want the mere act of opening your package to make her ill.

And finally, don't use your eBay business as a front for converting non-believers. By that I mean your packages really shouldn't contain political propaganda, Bibles, religious pamphlets, grass skirts, chicken bones, or anything else that may offend the beliefs of your buyers.

Escape it!

As distasteful (so to speak) as I found the enchilada box, the bra inside was fine. Thank goodness it was, because proving damage resulting from chili pepper residue would have been rather difficult. Unless there was a visible stain, about all I could have done was email the seller, explain the problem, and hope she was willing to accept a return.

Animal on Board

Some sellers like to include a little "bonus" in a package. A cosmetics seller may toss in a few samples of lipstick or someone who auctions scrapbook supplies may include an extra sheet or two of colorful paper.

But some bonuses are better left at home.

For example, there was the seller in Arizona whose package included a baby scorpion. Oh, it wasn't intentional—the little bugger just managed to get into the box when it was left open overnight in the seller's garage. Needless to say, the seller apologized profusely, but I'm not sure there are enough "I'm sorrys" in the English language to make up for that particular brand of surprise.

There was also the seller whose son's pet hamster stowed away inside a box. Thankfully it was alive upon delivery, so the buyer decided to have a bit of fun. He took the hamster on a "vacation" and then sent it back (more appropriately this time) with photos of the critter posing in various sites in the buyer's hometown.

One story of horror and one of humor, yet they both illustrate the same point: always check your package for tiny escapees before you seal it up and send it off.

Just Because It's Usable Doesn't Mean You Should Use It

Todd won an auction for a set of collectible baseball cards. They arrived packed in a Quaker Oatmeal canister with the original label intact. The shipping label and postage were affixed with tape directly to the box.

Although the cards arrived safely, Todd's mail carrier gave him a funny look when she asked him to sign for the package.

The actual buyer in this situation summed it up best: "I wonder what all the postal workers who saw this thought. I can just imagine them wondering, what idiot orders oatmeal and has it sent *priority mail?*"

Avoid it!

Here's the point to ponder if you're the seller: while an oatmeal canister isn't exactly embarrassing and is certainly quite sturdy, is it really necessary?

Baseball cards are small enough to fit into more traditional packaging, like a regular box or envelope and that would be a more appropriate choice. Pack these items with sturdy backing as discussed in the ""Do Not Bend" Does Not Work" section earlier in this chapter.

If the item is something that must be rolled up, such as a large art print or photograph, cardboard shipping tubes are widely available. But if you must use something like an oatmeal box, at least remove the outer label.

Bottom line is this: your packaging should pass unnoticed by delivery people and not cause your buyer to feel he has to explain himself. Or his oatmeal fetish.

Escape it!

As a seller, your packaging should be as plain as possible *and* it should be size-appropriate. Small items shipped in overly large boxes without insulation of some kind (such as packing peanuts) rattle around, increasing the likelihood of damage. A box that's too big may also needlessly increase the cost of shipping.

NOTE   If you buy something and it arrives with a postage sticker bearing a price far less than what you paid for shipping, you're pretty much out of luck. Once you bid on something, you're agreeing to the terms in the auction—so if it says the shipping is $10 but it cost the seller only $2 to ship, complaining about it is an exercise in futility. I discuss this more in Chapter 4.

When to Take Special Precautions

Although packaging items to avoid breakage (or embarrassment) is of paramount concern, there are some situations that require you to think ahead a bit more.

Items can arrive intact and still be completely ruined. It's your job to assume the worst will happen and package accordingly.

Batteries (Should Not Be) Included

Grace purchased a robotic toy for her grandson. It was one of those items sold out in all the stores so she was happy to find it. The item arrived and was, as the seller stated, new in the box. Grace wrapped the item lovingly (as only a grandmother knows how to do) and proudly presented it to her grandson on his birthday.

When he pulled the toy out of the box, there was battery acid all over the battery compartment and down the back of the toy. Apart from the obvious damage to the plastic caused by the acid, the toy was completely inoperable.

Grace contacted the seller, who told her he included the batteries "to be nice" and in light of his generosity, he didn't appreciate her ungrateful attitude.

Avoid it!

If you're the seller, never ship batteries inside a battery-operated item. They have a nasty tendency to leak during shipment, and battery acid pretty much destroys everything in its path. So if you're selling a used item, be certain the batteries have been removed prior to shipment.

If you're selling a new item, check the box for a "battery included" notation. Some manufacturers are selling items with the required battery already inserted (again, not a great idea), so be absolutely sure that's not the case before you ship.

If you want to go the extra mile for your customer and include batteries with the item, buy a new package and toss the sealed batteries into the shipping box. Your buyers will appreciate your thoughtfulness, and you won't have to worry about your good deed being punished.

NOTE   This also applies to toner cartridges being sent with inkjet printers. Take them out and seal them in a plastic bag before you put them in the box. Ink isn't something you want leaking all over the place.

Escape it!

If you're the buyer and you receive something with a battery acid leak, don't touch it. Take photographs and notify the seller.

Liquids Can Leak

Stephen purchased a beautiful Victoria's Secret silk nightgown for his wife—a present for their anniversary. Since the seller offered to combine shipping on multiple purchases, Stephen browsed her other items and found a bottle of his wife's favorite scented body oil. He purchased the oil as well, and the seller told him she'd be shipping both items in the same box and she gave him a shipping discount as promised.

When the box arrived, Stephen was horrified. The bottle of body oil had leaked all over the delicate silk nightgown, and the resulting stain was impossible to remove.

Avoid it!

As a seller, always put plastic or glass bottles in a Ziploc bag before putting them into the shipping box, especially if a bottle is being mailed with another item.

I've been traveling by air as long as I can remember, but I still recall my first lesson in Product Leakage 101. Due to the change in air pressure, a plastic tube of hair gel compressed, popped open, and oozed sticky goo all over my clothes. So there I was on my first day of vacation, scrambling to find a Laundromat since everything had to be washed before it could be worn.

I quickly learned to seal plastic bottles in Ziploc bags before tossing them into my luggage. It's a lesson I've carried forth into my selling practices on eBay, and you should too. Most items ship by air these days, and the air pressure in cargo holds can vary wildly. Plastic bottles have been known not only to leak, but also to completely burst in transit. Even bottles shipped by ground methods can break open from rough handling.

Escape it!

If you're the seller, you should always assume bottles will leak and take precautions to protect other items in the box. If the liquid escapes and ruins the other item, there's no escaping the fact that you have to refund the money or replace the items.

If you're the buyer of, oh say, a bottle of body oil, and 10 percent of it leaks out during shipping, you may be irritated that you're not getting the full bottle for which you paid (and that you had to clean up the container).

If this happens, email the seller immediately. Timing is important here. You don't want her to think you've tested the item first (which would account for the missing oil). Take photographs of the oily box and also one of the bottle, showing how much product is gone.

This is one of the rare circumstances under which I'd condone a seller giving a partial refund. Normally I advise against it (too many buyers try to get some of their money back on every item they purchase) but if 10 percent of the product is missing, a seller could offer to refund 10 percent of the buyer's money. It makes more sense than the product being returned for a full refund, unless that's what the buyer wants.

NOTE   If you've sold an item that was received partially damaged (or part of the contents leaked), you may want to issue a partial refund. If you received payment through PayPal, follow these steps: log onto PayPal, go to the payment transaction page for the auction, and click the "refund" link at the bottom. Specify the amount you want to refund to the buyer. You can do this for up to 60 days after your buyer made the original payment.

When You Shouldn't Ship at All

Lawrence auctioned off a large piece of leaded glass. It was extremely heavy and had been used as the top of a coffee table for which Lawrence no longer had the frame.

Once the item sold, Lawrence suddenly realized he had no idea how to ship it. He consulted a few glass companies but their packaging costs were wildly prohibitive, so he decided to try doing it himself using the tips provided by a kind glass-company clerk.

Despite an enormous output of time and energy, the leaded glass arrived at its destination cracked and unusable.

Avoid it!

A lot of eBay sellers get so heady with glee at how easy things are to sell that they forget the purchase of an item is only the beginning. You have to actually *send* the item too.

Some things simply can't be safely shipped without the help of a professional, which can be extremely pricey. You can certainly consult with a pro but do it *before* you list your item for sale so you won't be surprised by the cost later on.

NOTE   It is against eBay policy to ask a buyer to pay shipping costs above and beyond what's quoted in your
auction—so if the price of sending the item exceeds
that figure, you'll be on the hook to cover the difference yourself. Ouch.

Many people find the cost of shipping the item is much higher than
the value of the item itself, so they take a more sensible approach.
They specify the item as "local pick-up only" (Figure 3-5) and leave
it up to the buyer to transport the item home himself.

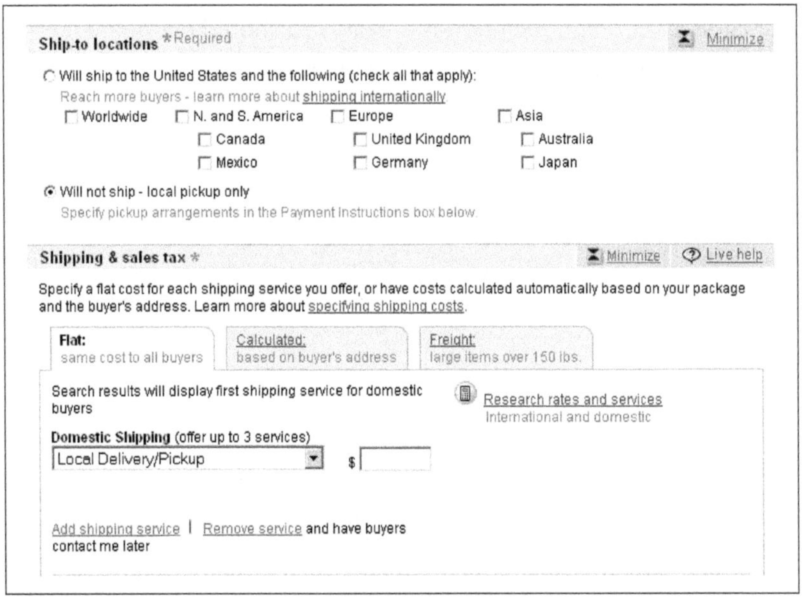

Figure 3-5. The shipping details section of the Sell Your Item (SYI) form. Select
"local pick-up" where designated.

This is often a smart choice for large, fragile items such as wall mir-
rors, leaded glass, neon signs, etc. You'll have fewer bidders but at
least you won't be responsible for shipping those unwieldy items.

"Local pick-up" is also usually the *listing* method of choice for people with furniture to sell. There are certainly crating companies who
are happy to pack up and ship such pieces for you, but the cost can

be prohibitive unless you sell a lot of furniture (and thus get a discount from the crating company).

NOTE   If you aren't sure whether it makes sense to ship your item, check out eBay's Freight Resource Center at *http://ebay.freightquote.com*. You can get packing tips and shipping quotes and create a "freight calculator" for use on your auction.

Sometimes you'll have better luck simply putting an ad in your local paper than you will selling the piece on eBay. Just because the newspaper isn't very high-tech doesn't mean you should eliminate it as an option. Going old-school is still sometimes the best choice.

4

Don't Get Burned on Shipping

So your widget is ready to go. Everything's nice and secure. You've used a good sturdy box and enough packing peanuts to simulate a Minneapolis snowstorm. Well done!

Now what?

Unless you're in dire need of frequent flyer miles and are planning to deliver the item in person, the next step is selecting a shipping service. And they *aren't* created equally.

For example, only one carrier accepts items sent to P.O. boxes. Another is best for lightweight items. One in particular charges international customers exorbitant fees for the privilege of delivery. There's a certain carrier that insists on a signature for any item delivered to an apartment building. All will be revealed in this chapter!

Other considerations: should insurance be purchased? Can the item be sent via air? What prohibitions do some foreign countries have against certain items?

Confused yet?

Well, don't be. It's a lot to remember but it's not as bad as it sounds and some details are pertinent only under rare circumstances.

I mean, how often will you want to ship chrysanthemums to Latvia, dried milk to Denmark, or underwear to Peru?

Assuming you just said "never" (and I really hope you did), you'll be able to absorb what's necessary from this chapter and refer back to the minutiae when necessary.

As your eighth-grade Social Studies teacher used to say, "It won't be on the test."

Pros and Cons of the Major Shippers

Dozens (if not hundreds) of shipping services exist, but for the purposes of this book, I'm going to focus on The Big Three: USPS, UPS, and FedEx.

All are reliable but each is better at some things than others. And sometimes you shouldn't trust any of them.

If you're an eBay seller, choosing the right shipper for your items can add to the excellent service you're already providing your customers.

And if you're an eBay buyer offered a choice of shipping services, selecting the most appropriate carrier for your new acquisition can save you money and untold amounts of aggravation.

Absolutely, Positively Overnight

Jeff, a resident of San Francisco, purchased tickets at a premium from a broker for the sold-out SF Giants/NY Yankees game.

A few days before the game, he learned he was going to be sent out of town on business so he decided to try to recoup his money by selling the tickets on eBay.

Since time was of the essence, Jeff ran a three-day auction, sold the tickets for slightly less than he paid for them and offered overnight shipping to his buyer (who lived in Las Vegas). The scheduling was a bit tight but the tickets were supposed to arrive that Thursday—the day before the buyer's plane would depart for San Francisco.

Unfortunately, Thursday came and went with no delivery.

Jeff frantically called the shipping company, who told him "mistakes happen" and that the tickets would be delivered the following day. But since the buyer had an 8 a.m. flight, this meant she'd have to depart without the tickets in hand and would therefore miss the game.

Jeff refunded his buyer and later spoke to the shipping company about their "on-time guarantee." He expected the carrier to cover the cost of the unused tickets since it was the shipper's fault the tickets hadn't arrived when promised.

You can imagine his horror when he learned he was only entitled to a refund of the shipping costs.

Avoid it!

If you're the seller, allow a week for your item to get where it's going, regardless of how it's shipped. If it has to be there sooner than that, you could be rolling the dice.

It's always risky to sell event tickets close to the date of the event, especially if your buyer lives out of town. Even the most reliable overnight shippers have a margin of error, and you can count on the fact that the mistake will happen at the most inopportune time. (Murphy's Law and all.)

It seems no one bothers to read the fine print of those "on-time guarantees" until something goes wrong, and only then do they learn that regardless of a carrier's incompetence, a refund of the shipping costs is all you're entitled to if they don't deliver when they said they would.

Ironically, if you purchase proper insurance, you're better off if the carrier takes gold in the Incompetence Olympics and just completely loses your package altogether. At least then you'll get a refund of the value of your item.

For tickets sold to out-of-town buyers, you're far better off arranging to meet them in person to complete the transaction, provided you will be in town yourself when they arrive.

If you're the Eek! a stranger!" type, take a big beefy friend along and/ or meet in a public place, like the buyer's hotel lobby or a nearby restaurant. And remember, cash only for a face-to-face transaction.

In Jeff's situation, he was going to be out of town when the buyer arrived, but he could have done one of a few things. An obvious option was to ask a trusted pal to meet the buyer in his place, collect the money and hand over the tickets. No muss, no fuss, no chance of the tickets being lost in transit.

Jeff also could have called the baseball park and possibly arranged to leave the tickets at the box office with the buyer's name and other identifying information. That way the buyer could pick them up herself the day of the game.

But if you're in Jeff's position and *must* ship overnight, I suggest FedEx (specifically their "Next Business Morning" service). Next-day deliveries are what the company was founded upon, and FedEx's record is better than anyone else's (although it's not as good as it used to be and UPS is a very close second).

> **NOTE**   The USPS's record for overnight shipments is less pristine, but it's significantly less expensive than FedEx or UPS and there's no extra charge for Saturday delivery. USPS also does something no one else in the business can: they deliver on Sundays and holidays.

Keep in mind: if you ship using a method that requires a signature upon delivery and no one's there to sign for the package, the courier won't leave it—which could ultimately result in a late delivery. If that happens, any guarantees previously issued for on-time delivery are nullified.

Escape it!

Sorry, if you're the seller, there's not much you can do but refund your buyer and do things differently next time.

Don't even *think* of just telling the buyer "tough luck" and sticking her with the now worthless tickets.

It may not be your fault the item wasn't delivered on time but it certainly isn't her fault either.

Why USPS is Best for International Shipments

Emma, a Canadian, purchased an item from an eBay seller in the U.S.

She paid the auction price and the stated shipping charges, but was surprised when UPS delivered her package and demanded another $50 in "brokerage fees"—this on top of the usual taxes Canadians pay on imported goods.

Emma was told if she didn't pay this fee, UPS wouldn't relinquish her package and would return it to the sender.

She paid it and then demanded her seller refund the fee. He refused, stating he had no idea UPS would tack on extra charges—and besides, she was responsible for knowing her own country's rules on these things.

Avoid it!

If you're buying from someone in another country, the only way to avoid brokerage fees is to have your item shipped via USPS or via air. If you're the seller, you may want to tell your buyer about the added fees so you don't end up in a battle with an irritated Canadian. (No, that isn't an oxymoron.)

Arguments over extra fees are a common problem between buyers and sellers who don't have much experience with international shipments.

It's a little complicated but let me try to walk you through it.

When you send something via ground shipment outside the U.S. and use a private carrier (that is, anyone except the USPS), you're asking the shipping company to be your representative and get those goods across the border. The shipping company basically takes on the role of "broker"—a person in charge of expediting the shipment through the customs office of the recipient's country.

The broker takes care of paperwork and makes sure the proper duties (a.k.a. taxes) are levied. The recipient is then expected to pay the broker's fee, which may or may not include the required duties.

So far it sounds fair, right? It stands to reason the broker should get a little something for his troubles. Call it a "handling fee," if you will (see Figure 4-1).

Here's the rub: those fees are usually based on the declared value of the item, but the percentage isn't regulated. So each carrier can charge what they want—and according to a lot of Canadians, UPS has a serious case of the greeds.

Canucks contend UPS's brokerage fee is outrageous, making it more expensive than other private carriers (like FedEx) who do the exact same job.

UPS's brokerage fee includes duties, but they're only a small portion of the grand total. The rest is UPS's own fee, and the exorbitant sum routinely charged for doing five minutes of paperwork should at least involve breakfast and a kiss goodbye.

Worse yet, when you ship with UPS, they don't tell you about these fees in advance so you won't even know you're about to have a *very* unhappy recipient on your hands. UPS won't release the package until those brokerage fees are paid. If the buyer refuses to pay, the package is returned to you, and you'll be the one paying for its scenic trip home.

WARNING   FedEx doesn't require its brokerage fees be paid upon delivery but it invoices for those fees later. If the recipient refuses to pay, the sender is ultimately responsible for those fees himself.

Rates for Customs Clearance into Canada

✦ Entry Preparation Charges
✦ Disbursement Fees

Entry Preparation Charges

UPS offers free[1] routine customs clearance of UPS Express Plus, UPS Express, and UPS Expedited. Our published rates are among the lowest in the business, with savings of up to 30 percent and often more. Use the chart below to calculate the customs brokerage fee for your inbound shipments.

Customs Brokerage Fee

Value for Duty	UPS Standard Service and All Other Couriers/Transportation Companies[2]	UPS Express Plus, Express, and Expedited Services
$0.00 to $20.00	$ -	Free[1]
$20.01 to $40.00	$6.90	
$40.01 to $100.00	$19.00	
$100.01 to $200.00	$28.30	
$200.01 to $350.00	$36.70	
$350.01 to $500.00	$41.20	
$500.01 to $750.00	$46.85	
$750.01 to $1,000.00	$52.40	
$1,000.01 to $1,250.00	$58.05	
$1,250.01 to $1,600.00	$61.70	
$1,600.01 to $5,000.00	$65.00	
Each additional $1,000	$5.10	

Disbursement Fees

Customers are responsible for payment of duties and taxes. When funds are not provided in advance by the customer, a fee of 2.7 percent (minimum $5.85) of the amount advanced by UPS will be charged. To avoid disbursement fees call 1-800-PICK-UPS and ask about our pre-payment and EFT plans.

Additional Services

Service	Charge
Each additional classification line after first 5 lines	$4.00/line
C.O.D. Fee for Collecting Brokerage Charges	$4.25
Release on Minimum Documentation (only non-UPS shipments)	$10.00 each
Import Permits	$23.00 each

Figure 4-1. UPS Customs Clearance fees for Canada: what you're seeing isn't even everything that's charged. Avoid these fees by shipping via air.

Case in Point

While some people feel it's unfair to single out UPS as the problem child, a quick Google search shows how numerous the complaints about UPS are.

- Results for "hate USPS": 236 pages
- Results for "hate FedEx": 1,240 pages
- Results for "hate UPS": 3,370 pages

Some of the most informative web sites about Canadian shipping:

1. Guide for Canadians to Ordering Online from U.S. Shops: *http://www.stokecity.ca/orderfromus.shtml*
2. Shipping with UPS from the States—BEWARE!: *http://www.dslreports.com/forum/remark,6938443*
3. United Parcel Service Sucks: *http://www.vcnet.com/~rossde/UPS_sucks/index.html*

How do you avoid these fees? There are a couple of simple ways.

- If you're going to send items (especially expensive ones) to Canada, do it by air instead of ground. The shipping costs are more but the buyer won't be hit with a bunch of extra brokerage fees later on.

- Ship via USPS. For all items valued under $1,200 Canadian, the recipient pays duties, taxes, and one flat $5 fee. This avoids the brokerage headache altogether.

NOTE   Many savvy Canadians won't even bid on auctions that don't offer USPS shipping.

Escape it!

As the buyer or seller, you may be able to raise enough hell with UPS to get at least part of their brokerage fees refunded, but it's an uphill battle on a mighty steep slope.

Sellers, if you're going to open up your auctions to international buyers, it makes good business sense to do a little homework and find out what the final cost to them will be. Unless, of course, you like receiving vitriol from another country.

And really, the U.S. gets enough of that without your help.

Buyers, if you don't know how your country handles shipments from outside its borders, you need to find out—or limit yourself to local sellers.

You can't really blame a foreign seller for not knowing the ins and outs of shipping to every single country on the planet. Do a little of the footwork yourself and you'll both be spared some unnecessary grief.

WARNING   It's bad form to ask a seller to lie about an item's value on a customs document just so you can save some money in duties. See the "When Honesty Is the Best Policy" section later in this chapter for more details.

Delivery Confirmation Is Not Tracking

Miranda sold an item on eBay, received payment via PayPal and used PayPal's shipping center (Figure 4-2) to print a USPS shipping label with *delivery confirmation* (DC).

She emailed the delivery confirmation number to her buyer and shipped the package.

A week later, her buyer emailed to say the package still hadn't arrived and when he used *http://www.usps.com* to track the package, there was no activity shown. It simply said the postal service had been "electronically notified" to expect the package.

He said if the package had actually been shipped, the web site would show in-transit scans. He accused Miranda of stealing his money and

Figure 4-2. PayPal's shipping service is fast, easy, and free (excluding postage costs, of course). Click the "ship" button next to any PayPal payment and follow the instructions. For more help, view the demo at https://www.paypal.com/shipctr/.

demanded to know where his package was, but she had no more information than he did.

The buyer then left scathing negative feedback in which he called Miranda a thief and a liar.

Two days after his rant, the package arrived safe and sound. A check of the DC number showed the date and time of delivery, but no prior information about the package's path en route.

Avoid it!

Buyers and sellers repeat after me: delivery confirmation is *not* tracking. Its only purpose is to show delivery (hence the catchy name).

There are two types of DC:

Retail DC
> Purchased at the Post Office. You've probably seen the neongreen label and its accompanying bar code on packages before.

Online DC
> A plain bar code appearing on shipping labels printed at home using one of several shipping services.

While the end purpose of both is the same (the bar code is scanned by the postal carrier when the package is delivered), what happens along the way can be vastly different.

Retail DC is typically scanned when postage is purchased at the Post Office. It's also often scanned en route to its destination so sometimes you can see the colorful journey your bag of organic catnip took before finally reaching you.

Online DC is usually *not* scanned when the package is dropped off. In fact, it's rarely scanned at all until the package is actually delivered.

Problems can happen when buyers accustomed to retail DC check an online DC number and see only this statement:

> The U.S. Postal Service was electronically notified by the shipper or shipping partner on March 15, 2006 to expect your package for mailing. This does not indicate receipt by the USPS or the actual mailing date. Delivery status information will be provided if / when available. Information, if available, is updated every evening. Please check again later.

To a nervous buyer, that looks like a very wordy way of calling him a sucker.

Online DC is relatively new so not everyone is used to how it works yet. And many people don't understand that while retail DC *may* be scanned en route, there's no guarantee of it since "tracking" isn't a promised feature of any form of DC.

UPS and FedEx have much nicer tracking capabilities—called "station to station" tracking—built right into their service. Within 12–24 hours after a package is accepted, you can check the web site to see where it is.

WARNING   Never leave a pre-paid UPS or FedEx package unattended on a courier's counter and just walk away, assuming it will be taken care of. Hand it to an agent and be sure it's scanned. If the package is stolen or lost before that first scan, the automatic insurance coverage provided by both companies is void.

UPS and FedEx also have detailed information about delivery (like the name of the person who signed for the package), whereas the USPS simply scans the package when the item reaches its destination. That can mean the package was placed in someone's hands or simply left on a doorstep.

I've also heard numerous stories of items scanned by the USPS as "delivered" when in fact they weren't. They were either on their way to be delivered (and later found in the carrier's truck) or the carrier felt uncomfortable about leaving the package unattended on a front porch and took it back to the Post Office.

Those types of scenarios pretty much never happen with UPS and FedEx. If they try to deliver and no one's home, that's noted in the tracking record. If they leave the package, the location is noted. Etc, etc, etc.

So if precise tracking capabilities are important to you, you should use UPS or FedEx instead of the USPS.

Escape it!

Sellers, when an antsy buyer contacts you with concerns about the DC number you've given her, politely explain that DC is *not* tracking.

If you've used online DC, also explain the difference between that and the retail DC with which she's probably more familiar.

NOTE   Some buyers practically watch the clock from the moment an item is shipped and email sellers in a panic if it's not received within a few days. It's good to let your buyer know that although the USPS states Priority Mail should take 2–3 business days to arrive, there's no guarantee. The wait can be much longer—and Media Mail (a.k.a. Book Rate) may be a month or more in transit.

Buyers, pay attention to which shipper the seller uses and adjust your expectations for package tracking accordingly. Select only sellers who offer shipping via UPS or FedEx if you absolutely must know the pinpoint-precise location of your package at all times.

And then see someone about your control issues.

Delivery Driver Responsibility

Alan purchased a feather bed from an eBay seller, paid for his purchase, and awaited delivery.

A week or so later, he returned from work to find one of UPS's yellow "delivery attempted" notes stuck to the front door of his apartment. The note stated a signature was required for delivery so Alan signed the note and put it back on his door before leaving the next morning.

He came home that afternoon to find yet another yellow note. On this one, the driver had written, "Unsafe to leave package unattended. Signature required in person."

Alan called UPS and asked if the driver could come by later in the day since she always tried to deliver his package at around 10 a.m. when he was already at work. He was told the drivers have a set delivery area and always start at one end and finish at the other.

Shipping from Home

A few years ago, you could ask sellers what they hated most and you'd hear "shipping" over and over again. The writer's cramp from handwritten labels and countless hours spent at the Post Office sucked the joy right out of selling on eBay.

For the most part, those days are gone. Several popular online services have streamlined the process so much that it's now almost effortless. All that's required is an Internet connection, a printer, paper, and some tape (to attach the label to the package).

PayPal's Shipping Center (see Figure 4-2) is integrated with the payment service. You can select USPS or UPS as the shipper, choose the level of service (Priority, Express, etc.), purchase delivery confirmation, insurance, and other optional services, pay for everything with your PayPal account, and print a professional shipping label onto a plain sheet of typing paper.

Aside from the cost of the shipping itself, the service is free.

The main limitation is that only items paid for with PayPal can be shipped using its service. And since the labels bear an eBay logo, some sellers feel this makes their packages more attractive to thieves.

Stamps.com and *Endicia.com* are both licensed by the USPS to sell postage on their behalf. The services work in much the same way. You download proprietary software (Endicia's works on PCs and Macs; Stamps.com's is PC-only) and for a flat monthly fee, you can print shipping labels, postage stamps, postcards, and such to your heart's content.

The upside to using one of these services is that no matter how someone pays you, you can print out a shipping label for the item purchased. Each service offers insurance through more than one company (in fact, Endicia has its own), which can make claims faster and easier.

The downside is the services cost money—monthly fees range from $9.95 to $34.95, excluding postage—and they typically allow shipping only through the USPS (the Premiere version of Stamps.com recently integrated FedEx shipping as well).

Aside from the obvious time-saving perks the services mentioned above offer, they'll also save you a bit of cash since delivery confirmation is free for items sent via USPS Priority mail and only 14 cents for other classes of mail.

—continued—

If you purchase postage at the Post Office instead, retail DC (see the "Delivery Confirmation Is Not Tracking" section earlier in this chapter) costs you 50 cents for Priority Mail and 60 cents for other classes of mail.

UPS.com and FedEx.com both allow you to sign up for an account online, then prepare and pay for shipments without any additional fees. You can drop off packages at a local customer service center or kiosk, or drop them into a company-branded drop box. Some U.S. Post Offices even have FedEx drop boxes in their facilities.

Investigate all the online shipping choices, evaluate your needs, and choose accordingly.

Unfortunately, his apartment building happened to be at the starting point.

Okay, then could the driver deliver the package on Saturday, when Alan wouldn't be at work? Nope. Saturday delivery costs extra and the sender hadn't paid for that.

The UPS supervisor asked if Alan had a neighbor with whom the package could be left, but they all worked the same hours he did. And he couldn't accept deliveries at work, so that was out.

Since Alan had no way to get the package, it was held for a week and then returned to the sender.

Avoid it!

If you're a buyer who lives in an apartment building, the only way to avoid this situation is to refuse to buy from sellers who use only UPS. If you're a seller, offer several shipping options. Hopefully your buyer knows what carrier works best for him.

Sometimes I think UPS spends nights and weekends thinking of new ways to alienate their customers. Why else would they have a set of policies designed to make people chase their tails?

Those of you who live in freestanding homes probably don't understand the fuss because UPS allows you to put a signature on file, and unless the sender specifically requests a signature upon delivery, your package will be left for you. Apartment-dwellers aren't so lucky.

UPS's official stance is that since apartments are so close together, the chance for theft increases exponentially.

Add to that the absurd policy of making their drivers responsible for packages that disappear and it's pretty much a given that anyone who works during the day and lives in an apartment building (without a doorman) is going to be wildly inconvenienced.

UPS may not have many packages stolen and for that, they should be commended. But a stellar safety record probably doesn't counterbalance the fact that many of us will simply use another carrier so we actually get a shot at having our packages delivered in the first place.

Alan's story is a meld of my own and that of several other people who've experienced the same frustrating scenario. To wit: I've lived in my apartment for years. I know the area and I know my neighbors. Packages left by FedEx and the USPS don't go missing around here so I have little reason to believe thieves would find those left by UPS any more alluring.

But what *I* think doesn't matter. My UPS driver seems to think my tiny beach town has a crime rate rivaling that of New York—so unless a package is small and flat enough to be hidden under my doormat, I have to be here to sign for it.

Alternatively, I can take time off work to go pick up the package myself at one of the service centers. If they were as ubiquitous as Post Offices, that wouldn't be a terrible hardship. But they're not.

My way of avoiding it is to simply refuse to buy from sellers who ship only via UPS.

And when I sell, I don't ship via UPS. I primarily use the USPS and sometimes FedEx. (Both are better than UPS about leaving packages.) I'm not going to take the chance of inconveniencing my customers.

Why You Should Always Offer USPS Shipping

It's a good idea for eBay sellers to offer their buyers a choice of shipping companies, and one of them should always be the USPS. I say that because USPS is the only carrier who delivers to U.S. Post Office boxes. You may be surprised how many buyers have them.

So if you use only UPS or FedEx, you're shutting out those bidders.

USPS is also the only carrier who can handle packages addressed to overseas APO (Army Post Office) or FPO (Fleet Post Office) addresses. When shipping from the U.S., the charge for it is no more than a regular domestic delivery. Many sellers even absorb the postage costs for items sent to APO/FPOs as a show of support for our troops.

It's a lovely gesture, one sure to generate a lot of good karma.

And does anyone ever have enough of that?

Escape it!

If you're a buyer stuck in UPS Hell, talk to one of your neighbors to see if she'll accept packages on your behalf (stay-at-home moms are good ones to ask).

Can you accept package deliveries at work? If so, you can reroute the package there instead. If you live in an apartment complex with a leasing office, someone there is almost always willing to sign for and hold your packages for you.

Otherwise, you'll have to rearrange your schedule and visit a UPS service center to pick up the package yourself.

Insurance Issues

Insurance is one of the most confusing aspects of shipping.

When an item is lost or arrives broken, buyers and sellers start pointing fingers at each other and screaming about who should eat the loss.

Many sellers feel if a buyer rejects insurance, he's taking his chances and the seller should therefore not be held responsible if something goes awry.

And buyers feel sellers are the ones in charge of shipping the package so it's up to sellers to insist on insurance if they don't want to be held liable should there be a problem.

Who's right?

As with almost everything else on eBay, it depends on the circumstances.

A Disclaimer and Two Bucks Will Get You a Cup of Coffee

Maggie is a seller of rare books on eBay. All her auctions bear the following disclaimer: "Insurance is optional, but I won't be held responsible for packages lost or damaged by the Post Office."

One weekend, she sold one of her expensive books. The buyer rejected insurance, so Maggie boxed up the book and sent it uninsured via the USPS.

When the book arrived, it was completely ruined. It appeared the box had been soaked at some point during shipment, so the book's hardback cover was warped and the pages were smeared. The whole thing smelled of mold and mildew.

Maggie refused to refund, citing her disclaimer and the buyer's refusal of insurance.

The buyer then filed a *Buyer Protection* claim with PayPal. They ruled that since the item was unusable, Maggie was required to refund—even though the book was in perfect condition when she sent it.

She was out not only the $400 purchase price of the book (and the shipping costs) but another $10 for PayPal's administration fees.

Avoid it!

If I were to guess, I'd say the most common misconception among eBay sellers is that a disclaimer like Maggie's protects them in the event an uninsured item is damaged or lost in transit.

Except for some very specific circumstances, it's simply not true.

I can't really blame people for being confused, though. The *Uniform Commercial Code* states one thing, PayPal states another, and of course eBay has a set of rules all its own.

Let's start with PayPal's rules, since they apply to the overwhelming majority of eBay transactions and thus supersede other policies.

PayPal has an advanced level of protection for buyers called the *Buyer Protection Policy* (BPP). It kicks in when someone purchases from a seller who qualifies for the protection by having a *feedback score* of at least 50 with a rating of 98 percent or better. Among other things, the BPP addresses disputes about the quality of items paid for with PayPal.

Boiled down, the BPP states items must arrive in the condition in which they were described in the auction. So unless a book is described as water damaged, it can't arrive that way or the buyer can file a claim and likely get his money back.

Insurance isn't addressed anywhere in the BPP. PayPal simply doesn't care whether or not insurance was purchased, and they certainly don't care if a seller tries to excuse herself from liability with a disclaimer.

This is why we in the *Answer Center* so often say insurance protects the *seller,* not the buyer.

Had Maggie insured the package, she could have refunded the buyer on her own (without PayPal's intervention) and then filed a claim with the USPS for reimbursement since the book was clearly damaged during shipment.

This would have kept her buyer happy—and saved Maggie $10.

Buyers should note that while the BPP kicks in only with sellers who qualify for it, that doesn't mean sellers who don't qualify are off the hook. If you're a buyer who's purchased from a non-qualified seller, you'll find it's harder to get a damage-related refund but you should still notify PayPal because they will examine your case.

That's a relatively new policy, and one PayPal doesn't advertise. In fact, PayPal's "help" pages specifically state they don't get involved in "quality issues" unless the BPP applies.

But sellers who otherwise qualified for the BPP were opting out of it to protect themselves against such claims, so PayPal found a way to close that loophole.

PayPal now requires sellers to jump through several hoops if they don't want to participate in the BPP (which is otherwise automatic to sellers who qualify)—and they still consider claims from buyers even if the BPP isn't in effect.

Okay, so that's PayPal's take on things. What about eBay's?

Since eBay is only a "venue" and doesn't handle payments directly, they can't force a seller to refund regardless of the payment method but they'll sometimes dig into their own (very deep) pockets to help you.

eBay's little-used *Standard Purchase Protection Program* (SPPP) has some rather strict guidelines, though. If you want eBay to cough up money when a seller won't, it ain't gonna be easy.

The bottom line is the SPPP won't entertain claims of damage or loss in shipping unless the buyer purchased insurance.

This detail isn't on the regular SPPP page at *http://pages.ebay.com/help/tp/esppp-coverage-eligibility.html*—that page simply states lost or damaged items don't qualify for the SPPP.

The insurance exception is buried on the "Shipping Concerns" page at *http://pages.ebay.com/help/confidence/isgw-fraud-shipping-concerns.html* (see Figure 4-3). The Shipping Concerns page clearly states that buyers wishing to file claims must have purchased insurance or they're outta luck.

Items that are lost or damaged during shipping are not eligible for the eBay Standard Purchase Protection Program programs unless you are the buyer and one of the following conditions apply:

- You purchased shipping insurance and the seller failed to insure the item.
- You purchased shipping insurance and you or the seller filed a claim with the shipping carrier, but the claim was denied due to poor packaging.
- You purchased shipping insurance and you or the seller filed a claim with the shipping carrier, and the shipping carrier awarded the seller reimbursement but the seller failed to send a refund to you.

Figure 4-3. The teeny tiny insurance exception to the Standard Purchase Protection Program. This is one of the few instances where insurance protects the buyer rather than the seller.

See, I told you they wouldn't make it easy.

> **N O T E**   While USPS insurance must usually be purchased as an add-on, UPS and FedEx shipments automatically have $100 of insurance coverage.

PayPal and eBay's policies cover just about every possible circumstance, but there are some federal rules you may want to know too. Check out the *Uniform Commercial Code* (UCC) pertaining to sales by going to *http://straylight.law.cornell.edu/ucc/2/*.

Just keep in mind that unless you plan to spend the tens of thousands of dollars it requires to take a case to trial in a federal court, most UCC rules won't apply to your eBay transactions.

For example, the UCC allows sellers to transfer "ownership" of items to buyers as soon as the items are shipped (thus releasing the seller from any responsibility for what happens during shipment), whereas PayPal considers the item to belong to the seller until the buyer actually *receives* it.

Some eBay sellers have tried to fall back on UCC rules when items are lost or damaged in transit, only to be met with peals of laughter from PayPal. It has its own rules and everyone who signs up for a PayPal account must agree to them—the UCC be damned.

Escape it!

If you're a seller in this scenario and the buyer paid with PayPal, there's no escaping this one. You may be forced to refund whether you want to or not.

Don't *ever* send anything without insurance if you aren't okay with refunding the cost of the item should it go missing or be lost in transit. Everyone has their own comfort zone for the amount they're willing to risk—mine is in the $50 range. Anything more expensive than that and I'll buy the insurance out of my own pocket to protect myself if I have to.

If you're selling an item and you know ahead of time it will fetch a high price, build insurance into the shipping cost and require the buyer to purchase it as a condition of the sale.

You're within your rights to do that, even if the insurance ultimately protects you instead of the buyer who shelled out the money for it. Just make sure you state the insurance requirement in your auction.

The cost of an education can be quite high. Don't learn this lesson the hard way.

When Honesty Is the Best Policy

Jacob sold a set of DVDs for the television show *The West Wing* to an overseas buyer.

The set consisted of the first four seasons of the show (when it was helmed by the brilliant Aaron Sorkin and before it became a pale imitation of the stellar drama it once was, but I digress), and the final selling price was $250.

The buyer paid via an international money order. She then asked Jacob to mark the item as a "gift" on the customs form and declare its value as $50 so she wouldn't have to pay as much in duties (which are a percentage of an item's stated value).

Insurance Claims 101

In the unfortunate event you're a seller and need to file an insurance claim, here are some pointers.

- Keep the buyer advised of what he needs to do. Insurance claims require the item's recipient to keep all the packaging materials used to send the item. The shipper will inspect those materials to determine how exactly the item was damaged (for example, a book soaked in transit would likely arrive in a damp box covered in water stains). Essentially, it's the inspector's job to figure out whether the damage was the fault of the shipping company or the sender. She'll be looking for signs of improper packaging or an indication the item was already damaged before being shipped.

  If the buyer throws away the packaging material before the carrier has the chance to inspect it, the damage claim will be denied.Until the claims process is underway, a buyer shouldn't return the item to you—doing so almost always voids the insurance coverage.

- A buyer who refuses to cooperate with an insurance investigation likely has something to hide. Most buyers are all too willing to take packages to the Post Office for inspection and they'll fill out any necessary paperwork to get an insurance claim underway. If a buyer drags his feet on this or in any way impedes the claims process, you're within your rights to refuse to refund until he has a change of heart.

  Even PayPal will take such circumstances into account when determining a Buyer Protection claim. Yes, PayPal wants to protect their buyers, but they also don't want the BPP used to defraud sellers.

- Once you've verified with the shipper that the inspection has taken place and all insurance forms have been properly filed, refund your buyer. Don't wait until you find out whether the claim has been approved—it doesn't matter. If the claim is denied for a reason such as poor packaging, you still owe the buyer a refund. He doesn't eat those losses. You do since you were the one in charge of packing the item properly.

  As long as you were conscientious, your claim will likely be approved and you'll get back the money you already refunded your buyer. So there's no reason to make him wait.

—continued—

- Insurance claims are sometimes denied even if you did nothing wrong. Shipping companies are never happy about admitting fault and may deny your initial claim as a matter of routine. If this happens and you're sure an item was damaged through no fault of your own, use the process each shipper has for appealing denials of insurance payouts. Appeals have a fairly high success rate. Sometimes the squeaky wheel really does get the grease.
- Stay informed. Shippers maintain web pages outlining their claims processes. Read them and refer back to them when necessary.
  - USPS: *http://www.usps.com/insuranceclaims/welcome.htm*
  - UPS: *http://www.ups.com/content/us/en/resources/service/claims/*
  - FedEx: *http://www.fedex.com/us/customersupport/express/faq/claims.html*

Jacob agreed and shipped the item via USPS *Global Express Guaranteed* (GXE) at the buyer's request (Figure 4-4). While expensive, GXE is very fast, includes $100 of automatic insurance coverage and is one of the only USPS methods that allows a foreign buyer to track a package.

The day after the DVDs were mailed, all tracking activity for them came to a halt. Jacob was later told they were either lost or stolen, so the USPS refunded him the cost of shipping plus $50—the value he'd declared for the package on the customs form.

Jacob's buyer was furious when he refunded only her shipping and $50 of her $250 auction payment.

She told him he was responsible for refunding her in full but he didn't see how that was fair. Why should he be out money simply because he did her a favor?

Avoid it!

Sellers, the way to avoid Jacob's situation is to be honest on the customs forms. Falsifying them is a very bad idea, and not just to avoid the above scenario. For starters, it's a crime. No, you probably won't go to jail for it, but that doesn't make it any less illegal. Okay, with

Figure 4-4. USPS Global Express Guaranteed offers service and protection normally unavailable for international shipments. Check it out at http://www.usps.com/gxg/.

that out of the way (sorry, I have a degree in criminology and can't help myself sometimes), let's examine some likely repercussions.

It's not uncommon for foreign buyers to ask sellers to mark items as gifts. I can't say I really blame them. If I had to pay a percentage of an item's value simply because it came from outside my country's borders, I'd probably want those numbers fudged too.

But here's a little-known fact... in many countries, Customs holds an item's recipient liable for any untruths on the forms.

The reason for this is fairly apparent. I mean, think about it. How often is the U.S. asked to extradite someone for filling out a customs form incorrectly?

In other words, it's much easier for Australian Customs to punish an Australian buyer than an American seller.

"Punishment" can include revaluation of the item (to a number that may wind up being even higher than the actual amount), fines, fees, complete confiscation of the item, and/or being voted off the island.

(Scratch that last part. Just seeing if you were paying attention.)

NOTE   I read recently that Canadian Customs is now sometimes using eBay to determine an item's value. Unfortunately the agents aren't very eBay-savvy, so they may assign a value simply because it was the amount an optimistic seller was asking (and never got) for a similar item.

Another problem, as illustrated in Jacob's tale of woe, is insurance coverage. If you send a $500 item and state on the customs form that it's only worth $75, you can't really insure it for its true value. (In most cases, the amount of insurance can't exceed what you declare the item is worth.) Even if you *could* get away with it, you'd raise the eyebrows of an awful lot of Postal and Customs employees.

The opposite is true as well. Don't try to overvalue an item just for the potential insurance windfall if the item disappears in transit. Shippers like to see proof of what something's worth before they start shelling out cash, and a printout of an auction page suffices.

They won't be very happy when you present them with evidence of an amount far less than the declared value and insurance coverage. Words like "fraud" are thrown around in such situations, so it's better to just avoid it completely. Be honest on your customs forms. If the residents of countries like Canada want to keep their free health care and gunless streets, they need to realize those things cost money and it has to come from somewhere, dammit.

If I sound bitter and jealous, it's only because I am.

Escape it!

Okay, back to Jacob.

There's no real escape for the buyer in this situation. Since the buyer didn't pay with PayPal, Jacob can't be forced to refund her money.

But let's be honest, he was just as willing to play fast-and-loose with customs as she was.

Some would say it's proper for him to at least offer to split the difference and refund half her money. That way they both lose out equally.

Others would say that's nonsense and the buyer was responsible for the debacle, so she alone should bear the brunt of the financial hit.

And still others would say the seller is responsible for the loss since he's the one who shipped the item the way he did.

I'll leave it up to you and your conscience to decide who's right.

Shipping and Handling

Even though there's only one story to illustrate the point, it gets a section all its own.

Why? Because not a day goes by on eBay's message boards without at least one buyer raising eight different kinds of hell because she feels a seller "gouged" her on shipping.

Sometimes it's true. Usually it's not.

But it's always the same story with just a few minor variances.

Let us begin…

Shipping Is Not Postage!

Debra purchased a new eye shadow compact from an eBay seller.

She thought the shipping price of $2.99 was steep but the seller was the only one on eBay with that particular brand and color of shadow, and Debra had been looking for it for a while—so she bid on and later won the item.

When it arrived, Debra was shocked to see the postage on the package was only $1.00.

She left negative feedback for the seller with a statement that his shipping charges were "outrageous" since the postage he paid was so much less than what he'd charged her.

The seller negged her back, and Debra feels she didn't deserve it.

Avoid it!

If you're a buyer, I want you to get out a pen and paper.

Sit down and write this: "Shipping is not postage. Shipping is not postage. Shipping is not postage." Write it 100 times or 1,000 times or however many times it takes for you to believe it. Because it's true.

People who've never sold on eBay usually don't understand the hidden expenses of shipping an item.

Unless you want your new end table to simply have a shipping label slapped on the leg before being tossed into a truck, you'll need to take into account everything that goes into getting an item to you safely and in one piece.

In Debra's case, her eye shadow was shipped in a bubble mailer via first class mail with delivery confirmation.

Bubble mailers cost about $1.00. High volume sellers buy them in bulk for much less, but the occasional seller usually just grabs one at the drug store and pays full price.

Delivery confirmation for first class mail costs 60 cents if it's purchased at the Post Office. If an online shipping service is used, it's only 14 cents (see the "Shipping from Home" sidebar earlier in the chapter) but again, the occasional seller usually does things the old-fashioned way.

So $1.00 + $0.60 = $1.60. That accounts for all but 39 cents of the postage "overage."

But since we all know gas costs as much as smuggled drugs these days, we can safely assume the seller used up 39 cents of it when he drove to the post office to ship Debra's item.

There you have it. That's where the "outrageous" overcharge went.

Those little extra expenses add up, don't they? But to hear some buyers tell it, they expect sellers to eat those costs themselves.

And strangely enough, when you ask one of those buyers if she paid exact postage last time she purchased from an online retailer like LL Bean or QVC, she'll say she doesn't know because she never thought to look.

Nearly all retailers charge a handling fee and it goes unnoticed. But eBay sellers are scrutinized much more closely (and usually unfairly) for the same thing.

Now, when I say certain allowances should be made for costs over and above postage, I'm obviously not talking about a seller who charges $100 to ship a tube of lipstick. That *is* outrageous, and something eBay calls *fee avoidance*.

But here's the thing... you should always know what the shipping costs are *before* you bid on something. They're usually stated in the auction.

NOTE   To make browsing a little easier, you can add a column to your eBay search pages that displays the shipping costs for each item shown. Go to the Advanced Search page, click the "Customize search options" link on the upper right, and click the "Customize display" tab at the top. Select "Shipping cost" from the left column and click the arrow in the middle to move it over to the right-hand side. Scroll down, click the "Save" button, and voila!

If you think the shipping costs for an auction are too high, don't bid.

If the shipping costs aren't on the auction page itself, email the seller to ask how much they'll be.

Again—are the shipping charges too high? Don't bid.

And if he doesn't respond to the question at all, don't bid. You don't want to be stuck with whatever arbitrary figure he comes up with after the auction.

My point is this: as the buyer, you're in *complete* control of how much you pay for shipping—as long as you read carefully and ask the right questions *before* you bid.

If you don't do that, you have no one to blame but yourself.

Sellers, if you want to avoid unfair negative feedback from uninitiated buyers, consider using stealth postage (Figure 4-5).

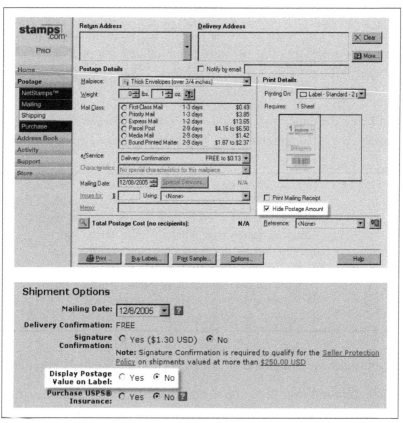

Figure 4-5. Stealth postage is one of the gods' greatest gifts to mankind (or at least to eBay sellers). Stamps.com requires a shipper to opt-in by checking a box, while PayPal has yes/no radio buttons. But don't gouge on shipping—use this power for good and not evil.

Stealth postage is a feature offered by online postage services (such as PayPal shipping, Stamps.com and some levels of membership on Endicia.com) that allows a seller to hide the amount of the actual postage he paid. The theory behind it is if the buyer didn't mind paying that amount for shipping when she bought the item, she shouldn't mind not seeing how much of it was spent on the postage itself.

It's a fabulous feature, one I use every time I ship. It simply takes the issue off the table. People can't complain about something they can't see.

You Can't Ship That!

The United States have a rather stringent set of postal rules. For example, you can't use the USPS to ship perfume by air. It must go via ground.

Why, you ask? Because pressurized air and flammable liquids can go "boom." And the USPS isn't a fan of the "boom."

Okay, so that rule makes sense.

But did you know you can't bring a lighter into this country unless it's deemed "childproof"?

Considering the young age at which most smokers take up the habit, I'm not terribly sure how effective a childproof lighter actually is.

Nevertheless, the U.S.'s rules for imports are actually mundane compared to those of some other countries.

The table below shows some items that are banned in other countries. Keep in mind, someone had to raise the issue of banning each of these things in the first place—and that person likely wouldn't have done so had there not already been an established pattern of a problem with the item.

It's up to your twisted imagination to conjure up what that problem is. Just don't do it in front of the kids.

You can't ship...	To...
Erasers resembling food in scent or appearance	Australia
Skimmed milk in tins	The Bahamas
Cards that play music when opened	Bulgaria

You can't ship...	To...
Margarine	Canada
Funeral urns	France
Panama hats	Ecuador
Melatonin	Germany
Playing cards	Greece
Blank invoices with headings	Israel
Musical instruments	Iran
Paper, envelopes, pens, pencils	Sri Lanka
Footwear of any kind	Syria
Japanese shaving brushes	Uganda

5

Don't Get Burned by Other eBayers

Ah, you thought it was just about money and stuff, didn't you?

No, cupcake. There are *people* behind the money and the stuff. And just like the people with whom you interact every day, the people on eBay can sometimes make things very, very difficult.

Perhaps their intentions are pure—and perhaps they're purely malicious—but you'll have to deal with the fall-out either way. It can be as minor as a smudge on your feedback record, or as major as the loss of your eBay account.

Save the Drama for Your Mama

Years of experience on eBay and countless hours spent reading the stories of others in the community forums have taught me this: some people have the ability to take a perfectly uncomplicated situation and make an utter mess of it.

It's a special gift, really. I'll bet you know someone who has it. And I'll bet you avoid him whenever humanly possible.

In case you were wondering, he spends his free time on eBay. I've bought from him and sold to him—and so have millions of other people. He's a busy boy, that one.

If you know the warning signs, you can sidestep him and the drama he brandishes like a sword.

That's where I come in.

I'm a big fan of drama-avoidance in general, especially when it comes to people I can't see. Nothing looks crazier than a woman muttering obscenities to a computer monitor.

So I go out of my way to be on the lookout for such things *before* they happen.

If all else fails, you can always stick pins in a doll named after the person. But that's so uncivilized.

You weren't raised that way.

Don't Be Quick on the Feedback Trigger

Leah, an eBay newbie, had rather high expectations from her first transaction.

She paid for her item and when it hadn't arrived a few days later, she immediately left negative feedback for the seller.

The seller, whose previously perfect feedback record had now been marred, was understandably upset. He retaliated and negged Leah back, leaving her with a feedback rating of (–1).

Leah tried to bid on other sellers' items but found herself blocked from them.

Frustrated, she signed off eBay and never returned.

Avoid it!

If you're an eBay seller, you probably whooped "Good riddance!" after reading of Leah's demise. Settle down.

Anyone who's spent time on eBay has surely run across auctions with *Terms of Sale* (TOS) stating newbie bidders aren't allowed. It's harsh and ridiculous—after all, without newbies, eBay would cease to exist.

But many sellers have been burned by the inexperience of people like Leah and are understandably gun-shy. All it takes is one clueless buyer to ruin years of flawless feedback.

For that reason, eBay's *Seller Preferences* allow sellers to automatically block bidders with a net feedback rating of (–1) or less. Even if that preference isn't set, most sellers cancel bids from people with such poor feedback ratings.

It's not personal—they just assume if you had trouble with your first transaction, you'll have trouble with others.

All this is fine and good for subsequent sellers who are protected after someone else took a hit and acted accordingly, but what about that first battle-scarred seller? Is he stuck with that bright, shiny neg?

Maybe not.

The *Mutual Feedback Withdrawal* (MFW) process (help → A to Z → M → Mutual Feedback Withdrawal) is one solution (Figure 5-1). If both the buyer and seller agree, the red donut that accompanies a neg (and the resulting impact on an overall feedback score) is removed.

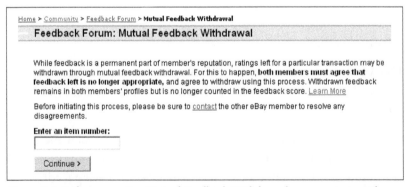

Figure 5-1. Before requesting Mutual Feedback Withdrawal, communicate with your transaction partner. Both of you must agree to the MFW or it won't take place (hence the word "mutual").

The comments they left for each other remain on their respective feedback profiles, but with time and additional eBay transactions, those comments eventually move off the first page of comments and thus are "buried"—meaning the casual observer has to really look to find them (though the total number of MFWs someone has are always shown at the top of every feedback page).

Some people have that kind of time (I envy them, don't you?) but most are just interested in an overall feedback score—not the comments attached to it.

If Leah goes through MFW, her score goes back to being (0). She may still have her bids canceled by sellers who refuse to deal with newbies (or sellers who read the neutralized feedback she left and received), but she can't be automatically blocked.

eBay very wisely doesn't have a system-wide setting to bar zero-feedback bidders. So the only way sellers can refuse to deal with newbies is to stay on top of their auctions and cancel bids as they come in.

Pretty tedious work, but it's difficult for a reason. Newbies are the lifeblood of eBay and eBay knows it.

For a very long time, MFW was the only way to deal with a situation like Leah's. But in June of 2005, eBay announced upcoming changes to the feedback system that could keep the whole thing from happening in the first place (see the "Feedback Fixes" sidebar later in this chapter).

One of the new policies requires a member with a feedback score of (10) or less to complete a tutorial before leaving neutral or negative feedback.

The tutorial urges members to allow enough time for each end of the transaction to take place, and also emphasizes the importance of communication with one's trading partner before leaving feedback.

And veteran eBayers rejoiced.

We've always assumed the main reason newbies are so quick on the trigger with negs is they simply don't know any better. Hopefully, the new tutorials (which are now in place) will provide a remedy for that.

The bottom line is this: there's simply no reason to leave negative feedback quickly.

No matter how green or grizzled an eBay member you are, you should use the tools eBay has in place to resolve disputes—and only *then* leave the feedback you feel is appropriate.

And remember, sometimes the best feedback to leave is none at all.

Escape it!

If you're in Leah's shoes, don't despair (unless they're really hideous shoes no one should wear, ever).

Obviously, learn from your mistake and vow abstinence from leaving negative feedback before doing everything to avoid it.

Once you've done that, apologize to your seller and ask him to go through MFW with you. If he refuses and leaves you with a poor feedback rating, you still have options.

NOTE   Don't bother with *Square Trade* (*http://www. squaretrade.com*). It's a third-party mediation site that used to be able to completely remove feedback, but all it can do now is exactly what eBay can—feedback withdrawal. So don't pay ST to do what eBay does for free.

Many people don't know you can abandon a username and get a new one. eBay IDs are tied to email addresses, not actual names, so all you need is a different email address. The rest of the identifying information (your name, address, etc.) on the new account can match the old one.

If you want to continue using your original email address and attach it to the new username, get a free email account (through Yahoo, Hotmail, gmail, etc.) *before* you register the new ID. Change the email address on the first username (the one you don't want to use anymore) to the new email address, and then register your second eBay ID using your original email address.

WARNING   If your username has been suspended by eBay, you're not permitted to register another until the first is reinstated.

So let's say you register another username but many sellers *still* cancel your bids because you have a new account and no feedback.

How are you supposed to build your feedback and prove yourself a reliable eBayer when no one will give you a chance?

Start looking for *Buy It Now* (BIN) auctions, which are easily found in most eBay Stores (found at *http://stores.eBay.com*), or click the Buy It Now tab at the top of any eBay search page (Figure 5-2).

Figure 5-2. Whether you're browsing by category or doing a keyword search for a specific item, the resulting lists of auctions have three tabs across the top. The default is to show all current listings, but you can narrow the list to show only Buy It Now items.

Read the auction page to make sure the seller has good feedback, takes PayPal, and doesn't have any silly prohibitions against newbies. Then simply click the BIN button, pay immediately, and you're done.

It's the easiest and fastest way to collect positive feedback—especially if you'd like to become an eBay seller. Most people are wary of sellers who haven't been buyers first.

Once you have a feedback score of at least (10), sellers are much more willing to accept your bids in a regular auction. And again, if you're looking to get into the wild and wooly world of selling on eBay, you'll need a feedback score of at least (10) to list your auctions using options like Buy It Now, etc.

Feedback Fixes

eBay's feedback process has been the subject of frequent criticism over the years, but overhauls have been few and far between. It wasn't that eBay was unaware of the system's shortcomings, but rather that the most commonly suggested alterations would have put one transaction partner at a distinct disadvantage. But it looks like eBay found a way around that. In June of 2005, the following changes to the feedback system were announced:

1. All feedback left by members who are indefinitely suspended within 90 days of registration will be completely removed. eBay believes these people were never truly members of the community and therefore their feedback, whether positive or negative, shouldn't count. (It's not retroactive, so it applies only to feedback left after the policy was enacted.)

2. Members with a feedback rating of (10) or less will be required to take a tutorial before leaving their first negative or neutral feedback. View the tutorial at *http://pages.ebay.com/help/tutorial/feedbacktutorial/intro.html*. Also, the page *all* members see before leaving negative or neutral feedback will be updated to emphasize the importance of patience and communication.

3. Feedback left by members who don't participate in eBay's issue resolution processes, such as the *Unpaid Item Process* (UPI) or the *Item Not Received/Significantly Not As Described* (INR/SNAD) process, will be "neutralized" (see Chapter 2 for more on the UPI process). For buyers, this means they must respond through the eBay system when a seller files a UPI against them (and/or they must file an INR/SNAD, if circumstances warrant) or any feedback the buyer leaves will have no impact on the seller's overall feedback score. The comments themselves will remain, but neutralized feedback will be marked with an administrative note from eBay.

   For sellers, this means the eBay and PayPal systems will be aligned and if a seller leaves negative feedback without first filing a UPI, that feedback will be neutralized. The comments will remain with a notation from eBay. This particular policy is currently in effect for buyers, and eBay anticipates applying it to sellers sometime in 2006.

All these policies are new as of this writing. There isn't a lot of information available about them right now, but there will be in the near future.

I'm Picking Up Some Transaction Interference

Kathie routinely bid on folk art featuring large orange cats. (I can't resist slipping in a picture of my orange cat here, Figure 5-3.)

Figure 5-3. Now see, kitties this cute deserve to go on wooden plaques and welcome mats. This one enjoys sitting in boxes less than half his size.

Since these were rather "niche" items, she found herself up against the same three bidders on almost every auction. *Bidding wars* were common.

Kathie emailed the other bidders to ask them not to bid early in future auctions, since it seemed to drive up the final auction prices.

The next auction closed without Kathie placing a single bid... because her eBay account was suspended.

Avoid it!

Kathie may not have meant any harm, but eBay has extremely strict rules against *transaction interference*.

Put simply, you're never permitted to email bidders to warn them away from a seller or to discourage them from bidding—for any reason.

NOTE   The policy against transaction interference also prohibits eBay members from contacting one another for
the purpose of completing a transaction outside of
eBay. This is partly to keep the possibility of fraud to
a minimum, and partly because eBay makes a lot of
their money from the cut they take of each completed sale. If the sale takes place outside of eBay,
they get nothing. Horrors!

If you're an eBay seller, you want to get the highest price for your
item, right? So several buyers conspiring to keep that from happening isn't very fair. That's why the rule exists.

Even if a seller has ripped you off in the past, you can't email his current bidders to warn them away from him. That may not make sense
to you, but think about it for a second. Anyone can say anything in
an email. If you don't know the person, how do you even know she's
telling the truth? How do you know she's not one of the seller's com-
petitors trying to cost him business? I've even seen situations where a
supposed "good Samaritan" warned someone away from an auction
only to bid and win the auction herself (and for a much lower price
since competition was scarce).

You have no way of knowing what someone's motives are, so take
any unsolicited "advice" from strangers with a grain of salt. And
then report them to eBay at Help → Contact Us → Report problems
with other eBay Members (see Figure 5-4).

As for the bidders Kathie emailed, they were all too happy to report
her. One less competitor for them! Boo-ya!

Escape it!

If your account has been suspended for something like transaction
interference, chances are good the suspension is temporary. Contact
eBay using the information in your suspension notice and see how
long you'll be in purgatory.

Figure 5-4. When you use the Contact Us page of eBay's Help section, select the most fitting general topic from the first page, and drill down to specifics on the following page. Finally, click the "Email us" link on the last page to fully explain the situation to eBay.

Once you're reinstated, keep your fingers off the *contact member* email links unless you're using them to directly facilitate an eBay transaction.

Next time the suspension may not be so temporary.

What's Your Preference?

Take a little time to set your preferences and eliminate angst. You can block specific people from bidding (if you've had trouble with a certain buyer) or stipulate that you do business only in your own country.

Duck, Dodge, and Block That Bidder

Jade, a computer wholesaler and eBay seller, auctioned off a laptop.

The auction ended with a winner, but during the following month the buyer ignored Jade's repeated invoices and requests for payment.

Jade finally filed a UPI, left the buyer negative feedback for non-payment, and relisted the laptop.

The following week, her deadbeat bidder suddenly resurfaced and began winning all of Jade's Buy It Now auctions. In addition, four brand-new, zero-feedback bidders began emailing her with rude questions and later won many of her other auctions. All the bidders left negative feedback for Jade as soon as the auctions closed, and all of them ignored her requests for payment.

The mess cost Jade an enormous amount of money in *listing fees* and her feedback took a disastrous hit.

Avoid it!

The damage one disgruntled bidder can do is fairly catastrophic. Fortunately, there are ways to sidestep at least some of it.

One of the first features with which an eBay seller should familiarize herself is the *Blocked Bidder List* (BBL). Go to Help → A to Z → B → Blocked Bidder List (Figure 5-5).

People named on your BBL can't bid on your auctions. If they try, they'll get a system-generated page telling them their bids have been rejected. Anytime you have trouble with a non-paying bidder, add them to your BBL. In fact, you can add a person with whom you haven't even had trouble yet. Has someone emailed you a question you find odd or offensive? Add them to your BBL.

The BBL can sometimes go hand-in-hand with the Cancel Bids feature. To cancel bids, go to Help → A to Z → C → Cancel Bids (Figure 5-6). If you have a current bidder you don't like for any reason, cancel his bids and add his name to your BBL.

WARNING   Just adding someone to your BBL doesn't automatically cancel her bids. You must cancel them separately. And keep in mind bids on completed auctions can't be canceled.

Blocking a bidder/buyer:

Enter the User IDs of the eBay members you wish to block in the box below and click the Submit button.

Note:

- Separate User IDs with a comma, semicolon, blank space, or use the Enter key.
- You can block up to 1000 User IDs

Removing a bidder/buyer from your "blocked" list:

In the box below, delete the User ID(s) you wish to remove from the list, and click the Submit button.

Note:

- Inform the eBay members after lifting the block so that they can resume bidding on your items.

Blocked
Bidder/Buyer
list:

View an example of how to add or remove bidders/buyers from your list.

Submit

Figure 5-5. You can block up to 1,000 bidders by using the Blocked Bidder List. But if you're having trouble with that many people, it may be time for a little self-examination.

Canceling bids placed on your listing

Bids should only be canceled for good reasons (see examples). Remember, canceled bids cannot be restored.

Enter information about your listing below and click Cancel Bid.

123456
Item number

ImADeadbeat
User ID of the bid you are cancelling

Reason for cancellation:

Bidder's username is giving me pause
(80 characters or less)

cancel bid   clear form

Figure 5-6. eBay gives a generic list of "good" reasons to cancel bids, but you can safely ignore them. It's your right as a seller to cancel any bid for any reason—but remember it could cost you business if other bidders avoid your auctions because they think you're unreasonable.

And when I say "any reason," that's what I mean. It could be his feedback, it could be the other items on which he's bidding, it could be his username has "Yankee" in it and you're a Mets fan. You'll look a little nutty if you routinely cancel and block bidders for that last reason (and it may lower the bid price on your listing), but hey, it's your prerogative.

Just keep in mind any bids you cancel (and the reason you give for canceling them) are listed at the bottom of the *bid history* page for that auction, so don't get too wacky. It'll spook other bidders. No one wants to buy from a crackpot.

My point, though, is that you should listen to your instincts. The best way to avoid trouble is to avoid troublemakers.

For example, if all the feedback a bidder has left for other sellers shows he's impossible to please, you don't have to deal with him—as long as you use your magic wand to make him disappear *before* he wins your auction.

Bids can't be canceled after an auction closes, so it's a good idea to keep an eye on your running auctions if you can. Some sellers have far too many listings to baby-sit, but for most sellers it's a fairly manageable task.

And by all means—if you have an issue with a non-paying bidder (NPB), watch your listings like a hawk for the next week or two. NPBs have a rather remarkable capacity for revenge.

I know some sellers who had to get rid of Buy It Now auctions for several weeks simply to avoid the wrath of an NPB who would otherwise ruin every auction the seller had.

It's a shame someone can string you up like a piñata and take potshots at you when he's the one at fault. It's not common but it does happen, and you should be prepared for it.

Escape it!

Believe it or not, there *is* a little good news for Jade.

One of the (very few) reasons eBay completely removes feedback is if someone wins an auction for the sole purpose of leaving negative feedback.

Since the negs Jade received were left so quickly after the end of each auction, it was clear the bidders weren't on the up-and-up. She should report them at Help → A to Z → F → Feedback Abuse (Figure 5-7).

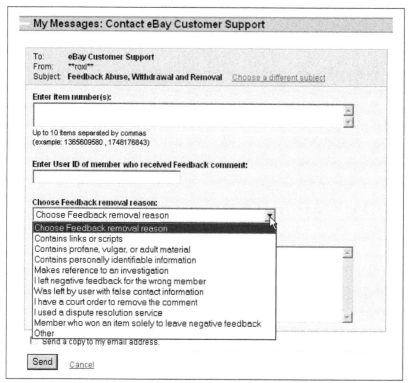

Figure 5-7. The Feedback Abuse form allows you to choose one of several reasons why the offending feedback should be removed. You can also explain the circumstances.

Furthermore, Jade can ask eBay to investigate all those new IDs to see if they're connected to the original person with whom she had trouble. eBay has all kinds of nifty investigative tools to smoke out such things. If the original bidder (or a friend or family member— yes, there are ways to prove that as well) created the other IDs, he'll be permanently suspended, as will all of his alter-egos.

Jade can file UPIs to get her *final value fees* (FVF) back from all the ruined auctions as well, but she's still responsible for the listing fees (and a relist credit as well).

Get to Know Your Seller Preferences

Gary's Buy It Now auctions for expensive jewelry clearly stated he ships only within the U.S. But foreign bidders continuously over-looked or ignored this, completed the BIN, and expected Gary to ship to them.

He always politely explained his rule about U.S.-only shipping and relisted the item, but the FVFs for all those pricey unpaid-for items began to add up. On top of that, he was paying listing fees twice on each auction.

The total amount finally got so high that Gary couldn't afford it, and his selling account was suspended for non-payment.

Avoid it!

One of eBay's Seller Preferences would have kept this from happening (see the "Preferences Are a Seller's Best Friend" sidebar later in this chapter). To wit: you can block bids from people who are registered in countries to which you don't ship. So if you're a U.S. seller and you select "U.S. only" when listing an auction, bids from everywhere else won't be accepted by the system.

Pretty simple, actually.

Also, when you're listing your item, you can set your BINs to require immediate payment—meaning the auction won't end unless the item is paid for via PayPal right then and there.

Just remember, you can't accept bids from people who want to pay with checks or money orders if you set up your BINs that way. But it certainly eliminates the possibility of non-payment. .

Escape it!

A foreign buyer who does a BIN on a U.S.-only auction is considered an "unwelcome bidder," and you can take steps to immediately recoup FVFs.

If you're the seller, you usually need to wait seven days after the end of an auction to file an *Unpaid Item Report* (UPI) and another seven days to close it, but there are two circumstances under which you can file/close immediately. One is if the buyer has been suspended by eBay (or NARU'd). The other is if she's registered somewhere other than where the seller specified he'd ship when he listed his item.

NOTE   Statements within an auction about where the seller will and won't ship aren't recognized by the system. The seller must make specific selections in the "Seller Ships To" section of the *Sell Your Item* (SYI) form when listing his item.

So file the UPI, select the reason for the filing, and close the UPI right away.

Two things will then happen. First, you get your FVFs refunded immediately. And second, your buyer gets an *Unpaid Item Strike* (UIS). Too many of those in too short a time and eBay will kick her to the curb. This may seem harsh, but a strike is deserved punishment for not paying attention to the terms of an auction.

NOTE   Sellers, don't bury your terms in tiny print at the bottom of an auction. While buyers are supposed to read the entire page before bidding, having clearly written, prominently displayed *Terms of Sale* (TOS) avoids confusion and may ultimately reduce your overall number of non-paying bidders.

Once you've done all this, you qualify for a relist credit (see Chapter 2)—so by the time all is said and done, the entire experience may have cost you a little time and aggravation, but not a lot of your hard-earned money.

Set your Seller Preferences accordingly to keep it from happening again!

Beware of Fakes and Friends

Trouble can come from any direction. You know there are thieves out there ready to take your cash, but you don't expect to lose money helping a friend. It's easy to stay flush (and popular) if you know what precautions to take.

The Vengeance of VeRO

Antonella desperately wanted the new Louis Vuitton handbag. She did *not*, however, want to pay the $5,000 for which it was retailing. Since she'd gotten so many great bargains on eBay before, she thought it would be the perfect place to find the bag at a discount. She was delighted to find the purse she wanted with a BIN price of only $500. She purchased it and paid immediately through PayPal.

Several days later, she received a notice from eBay that the auction had been pulled for a VeRO violation and she shouldn't pay for it. But since she already had, she didn't know what to do.

And what on earth was a VeRO? It sounded like a tragic baby name or a recalled car.

When Antonella hadn't received her bag a few weeks later, she logged back into eBay and saw her seller had been NARU'd. She filed a complaint with PayPal, who found in her favor, but by then the seller had already cleaned out his account and was long gone.

Preferences Are a Seller's Best Friend

Buyer Requirements Exemption List

You can allow specific eBay members to buy from you regardless of any buyer requirements you've set. Enter the User IDs or email addresses of the eBay members you want to exempt from buyer requirements below. When you're done, click the **Submit** button.

To remove an eBay member from the buyer requirement exemption list, delete the appropriate User ID or email address below and click the **Submit** button.

eBay members exempted from your buyer requirements:

Separate User IDs or email addresses with a comma, semicolon, or blank space.

Submit

If you're an eBay seller, you should get very cozy with your Seller Preferences. You can find them on your *My eBay page* under My Account → Preferences.

Under Selling Preferences on the next page, look for Buyer Requirements and click the "show" link. If you don't like what you see, click "edit."

You'll have the option to:

- Block buyers in countries to which you don't ship.
- Block buyers with an overall feedback score of (–1) or less.
- Block buyers who have received 2 unpaid item strikes in the past 30 days.
- Keep buyers from bidding on too many of your items in a certain period of time.
- Block buyers who don't have PayPal accounts.

Keep in mind you can always make exceptions for individual buyers by adding them to your *Buyer Block Exemption List (BBEL)* at *http://pages. ebay.com/services/buyandsell/biddermanagement.html.*

This is handy if, for example, you get a foreign bidder who emails you first to ask permission to bid on your U.S.-only auction. If you agree, you'll need to add his username to your BBEL or the system automatically rejects his bids.

—continued—

Keep in mind that although PayPal account holders are much less likely to be non-paying bidders than everyone else, if you select the option to accept only their bids, you're essentially shutting out people who can pay only with a check or money order—and newbies who may not have a PayPal account yet.

It's up to you whether you want to make those restrictions. One of the nice things about Seller Preferences is it puts *you* in control!

Avoid it!

There's a reason "greed" is among the Seven Deadly Sins.

A whole lot went wrong here. Let's break it down.

First off, eBay is lousy with counterfeits. Fake purses, fake jeans, fake jewelry. They're everywhere. If a well-known designer can make it and slap his name on it, rest assured it's being counterfeited and sold on eBay. Yes, of course there are rules against it, but that doesn't mean it can't happen.

Remember that the only way eBay knows an auction violates policy is if it's called to their attention. If they hired the manpower necessary to monitor each and every auction, they could single-handedly wipe out unemployment in the U.S.

So don't think that just because an eBay auction exists, the item within must be authentic. Even if the seller uses the word "authentic."

Since it's such a massive problem, many companies belong to an eBay body called VeRO—an acronym for *Verified Rights Owner.*

NOTE   eBay offers a policy tutorial about VeRO at *http:// pages.ebay.com/help/tutorial/verotutorial/intro.html.*

VeRO members have special privileges. If they see an auction that violates their rights in some way, they can ask eBay to remove it and eBay has no choice but to comply.

Some VeRO members—especially the high-end designers—have staff specially trained to spot fakes. These people are so good they can just look at a photograph and immediately tell if the item is authentic. If they happen upon a fake while the auction is live, eBay pulls it right then and there.

But sometimes things slip through the cracks and the fake isn't noticed until after the auction is already over, so that's when the auction page is pulled from the system.

Now, a quick lesson about counterfeits.

You'll never be able to buy a brand-new, in-season, authentic $5,000 Vuitton handbag for $500. Nor will you be able to buy a $500 Tiffany bracelet for $50. Or $200 Seven jeans for $20. Never. Never ever, in fact. Big-name designers don't wholesale their items to independent sellers. So when that eBayer says she got a "great deal" on Chanel bags from her wholesaler, you may rest assured her merchandise came from the trunk of a car.

WARNING   Don't be dazzled by authentic touches like dustbags, authenticity cards, tags, or receipts. A huge underground market exists to make those items, with the sole purpose of convincing you that a fake is real.

Besides, if the seller had a receipt for an authentic item she purchased herself, she'd be returning the item for cash or a store credit. She wouldn't be selling the item for a huge loss on eBay. Common sense, people. Don't let that $75 pair of Jimmy Choos make you lose your mind.

Does this mean every single designer item on eBay is a fake? No, of course not.

There are simple litmus tests you can perform to increase your chances of getting the real deal (see the "Filtering Out the Fakes" sidebar later in this chapter).

> **N O T E**   If it's designer handbags you seek, My Poupette (at
> *http://www.mypoupette.com*) is a terrific resource for
> information, photos, and advice about spotting and
> avoiding fakes.

If you want to be 100 percent certain of what you're buying, you'll
have to grit your teeth and purchase the item retail. And then get
your head examined for dropping five Gs on a freakin' purse.

> **WARNING**   It's illegal not only to sell counterfeit merchandise,
> but also to buy it. So don't stock up simply because
> the items look "good enough" to pass for real with
> your friends.

Having said what I have about counterfeits, I should also tell you
VeRO pulls auctions for other reasons, too. Since its main goal is to
protect intellectual property, even using a VeRO member's name in
an auction title could violate policy and get the auction yanked. This
means you can't list a pair of sunglasses as being "Chanel-like."
Unless Chanel made the sunglasses, you can't use their name in your
auction title at all. You also can't put a store name in your auction
title unless the item is an exclusive brand of that store (and sold
nowhere else).

> **N O T E**   Using terms such as "Gucci-like" or "Gucci inspired"
> in your auction title also violates eBay's rules against
> keyword *spamming*—but you *can* make one compar-
> ison to the designer item in your auction descrip-
> tion, as long as it's clear that item isn't what you're
> actually selling. See the rules at *http://pages.ebay.
> com/help/policies/keyword-spam.html*.

I recently bought a Philosophy skin care item from a seller who originally purchased it from the TV-shopping channel QVC. She put

QVC in the auction title and eBay pulled the auction when QVC (a VeRO member) complained.

Some VeRO members simply don't want their items on eBay at all.

Cosmetics giant Mary Kay, Inc. forbids its consultants (or ex-consultants) from selling its products on eBay. The rule is stipulated in the contracts consultants sign when they join the company.

Mary Kay also goes after non-consultants. They say there's no way to guarantee the "integrity" of the product unless it's purchased directly from one of Mary Kay's consultants, so they invoke their VeRO rights to pull the auctions.

Now, just for giggles, go to eBay and do a search for "mary kay." You'll find thousands of current listings.

Mary Kay's enforcement team can't be everywhere at once. But given its bulldog-like reputation for these things, it certainly tries.

Filtering Out the Fakes

Want a quick, easy, and (almost) foolproof way to tell if something on eBay is fake?

Look at the seller's other items for sale.

Does she have dozens of brand new, in-season and supposedly authentic designer pieces? If so, how do you suppose she got them? Did she knock over a Neiman Marcus?

That would probably make the news.

Are her Buy It Now prices ridiculously low? No sane seller is going to sell authentic high-end items for $19.99.

If either of the above applies, the stuff is fake. Trust me. Move on.

Does she have just one or two slightly-used items with starting prices of around half the retail value?

They're probably real. You may proceed.

Escape it!

If you receive notification that VeRO has pulled an auction on which you've bid, no further action is required on your part. The same applies if you've won the auction but not yet paid. Don't listen to a seller who demands payment.

Auctions pulled by eBay should be treated as though they never existed. UPIs can't be filed on them and feedback can't be left after the auctions are zapped, so any threats a seller may make are empty ones. But if the auction is over and you've already submitted payment, you should immediately file a complaint with PayPal (assuming that's how you paid). This often freezes the seller's PayPal account and any funds currently in it.

You'll likely win the complaint and the seller will be forced to refund your money—but there's the possibility of a snag. If the seller decides to abandon ship and lots of other people file complaints too, PayPal has a first-come, first-served policy for awarding refunds. Make sure you're at the top of the list by filing quickly. If you paid with a personal check, call your bank to inquire about putting a "stop payment" on it. Money orders can sometimes be canceled as well (except for USPS Postal Money Orders), so if you paid with one, call the company that issued yours to find out what your options are.

How to Sell for Others (and Retain Your Sanity)

Daryl was a regular seller on eBay with perfect feedback.

A friend of his received two iPods for her birthday. She had no experience with eBay so she asked Daryl to sell one of the iPods for her. He agreed and listed the item. The auction closed a week later. Daryl called her to ask when he should pick up the iPod for shipping.

His friend told him she'd sold the item to someone at work a few days earlier. Daryl was furious. She didn't understand why he was so upset. After all, if she could get a better price elsewhere, why should she have to follow through on the eBay transaction?

Daryl tried to explain what happened to his winning bidder, but the person wasn't very understanding. The bidder filed a report against Daryl for seller non-performance and left negative feedback.

Avoid it!

Many eBay sellers will tell you it's always a bad idea to sell things on eBay for someone else. Tales of woe abound about ruined friendships and family members who no longer speak to one another.

Here's what I say to that: if they had so much trouble, they either had incredibly bad luck or they weren't doing it right. I've sold for friends and strangers with absolutely no problems at all. Am I a masochist? No. Just meticulous.

Selling on eBay is a skill. Sure, anyone can become a seller, but there's a learning curve if you want to do it well. It takes experience and know-how to get the very best price for an item and finish the transaction smoothly.

In the past few years, hundreds of "eBay re-sellers" have popped up. You've probably seen a few. If selling for others is such a horrific idea, how are those companies surviving?

I'll tell you how. They're smart about it.

I like to think I am too, so let me tell you how it's done.

First, don't even bother trying if you aren't a *very* experienced seller. You should have all the basics down pat—how to research the best starting price, what an item is likely to sell for, how to take the best photos, and how to write the most effective item description.

NOTE   If you need someone to sell your items for you, an *eBay Trading Assistant* may be the answer to your prayers. Find one in your area by going to *http://pages. ebay.com/tradingassistants/hire-trading-assistant.html*.

If you're confident you have what it takes, the next step is to meet with your friend (family member, co-worker, etc.) and find out what they want you to sell.

Quite frankly, some things aren't worth your time. Many of the big re-sellers accept only items they know will sell for at least $50.

Examine the item for damage that will make it unattractive to bidders. This is where being an experienced seller comes in handy. You'll know which flaws matter and which ones don't.

If you decide to accept the item, you need to have a chat with your friend and lay down some rules. These are non-negotiable because they'll keep you out of trouble.

- Ask questions about the item. How old is it? Is there an interesting story about it? What was its original value? Who was the manufacturer? You don't want to sell anything if you don't know exactly what it is. Take notes.

- If the item is at all mechanical or electronic in nature, test it to make sure it works. Does your friend have the owner's manual? You want to make sure all the features operate correctly, so ask your friend to walk you through any buttons and switches.

- Ask your friend what the absolute bare minimum is he'll accept for the item. Write it down.

- Negotiate your fee. Will it be a flat fee or a percentage of the final selling price? Will you take your cut before or after any eBay and PayPal fees? Who's responsible for those fees? If the item doesn't sell, who'll pay the listing fees? Put it in writing.

- Add a brief statement explaining an eBay sale is binding. Be sure your friend understands he can't just change his mind and refuse to sell the item after the auction is over.

- Make a list of everything you're going to be selling along with the above details. Sign it, and have your friend sign it. Make a copy for him and keep the original yourself. (And if you're going to sell for others on a regular basis, draw up a standard contract—it'll make things much easier if you have a pre-printed form and you only have to fill in the pertinent details.)

- This is probably the most important rule: *Take the item with you.* Never sell anything you don't have in your possession.

You'll need to take photos, write the item description, and make sure nothing happens to it. Following this rule also eliminates the possibility of having the item sold out from under you.

- List the auction under your eBay account. Provided you've kept your password a secret (and you absolutely should), you'll prevent anyone else from being able to make changes to the auction without your knowledge.

- In the auction, stipulate the buyer must purchase insurance. Otherwise, if the item breaks in transit, you'll be responsible for refunding the buyer and reimbursing your friend for his now-broken item.

- After the auction is over, accept payment yourself. You have the item, so you're the one who should be paid.

- Package and ship the item yourself.

- Pay your friend when you know the item has been received and the buyer is satisfied—or after a reasonable period of time has passed for complaints. You don't want to be issuing refunds out of your own pocket if something has to be returned.

And there you have it.

Can things go wrong? Of course. But if you follow the steps detailed above, you'll eliminate nearly all the problems and misunderstandings that seem so common when the process is done carelessly. Bottom line: if you aren't comfortable with every required step, don't undertake the task at all.

Escape it!

Back to Daryl.

He tried his only available escape-hatch—begging for his buyer's mercy. It didn't work, so now all he can do is take note of what he did wrong and not do it again.

And take his lousy friend off his Christmas card list.

6

Don't Get Burned
by Scammers

Eleanor Roosevelt once said, "No one can make you feel inferior without your consent." By the same token, no one can take advantage of you without your express permission. If you've been the victim of a scam on eBay or PayPal, you probably screamed about the sites having been "hacked." That's a common cry but it's simply not true. Both sites are essentially bulletproof.

Trust me when I tell you scammers would much rather hack a web site than wheedle information out of people one at a time. If they could gain access to the financial details of millions of eBay or PayPal customers all at once, they would—but it's just not that easy to do. So scammers are forced to rely on the ignorance of the general population, something that can never be overestimated.

And thus, they flourish.

Buyers are usually the ones scammed, but there are times when sellers take hits too (albeit in much different ways).

You'll never get burned by scammers if you avoid falling into their traps. And this chapter is designed to keep you out of their slimy, scheming clutches.

Let's play the feud!

When to Be Afraid of Your Email

Your inbox should be a happy place. Unfortunately, some killjoys will go out of their way to turn it into a minefield. Read on and tread lightly.

Gone Phishing

While checking her email one day, Lola found a rather ominous looking missive from eBay. It said there had been some suspicious activity on her account, and the only way to keep it from being suspended was to update all her financial information. The email included a link to a web page where she could do that.

When Lola clicked on the link, she saw the familiar eBay logo in the upper corner and filled in the blanks for her personal information, including her bank account, credit card, and Social Security numbers. She thought it was odd that she was also asked for her mother's maiden name. She didn't recall being asked for that when she signed up for her eBay account, but maybe it had just slipped her mind. Satisfied she'd saved her eBay membership from certain doom, Lola finished filling out the form and turned her computer off.

A few weeks later when she received her credit card statement, she was stunned to see several large purchases she didn't make. When she called her card's customer service department, she was told the purchases triggered a fraud alert but the person making the charges knew her name, address, Social Security number, and mother's maiden name, so the charges had been approved.

Lola also began to receive statements for credit cards she didn't even have. The person who filled out the applications knew everything necessary to take the cards out in her name. By the time the mess was untangled several months later, Lola's bank account had been drained and her credit was ruined.

Avoid it!

Lola fell victim to something called *phishing*. It's one of the most common scams out there. See Figure 6-1 for a sample scammer email.

Dear valued eBay member

It has come to our attention that your eBay billing updates are out of order. If you could please take 5-10 minutes out of your online experience and update your billing records you will not run into any future problems with the online service.

Once you have updated your account records your eBay session will not be interrupted and will continue as normal. Failure to update will result in cancellation of your account, Terms of Service (TOS) violations or future billing problems.

To update your eBay records click here:

https://signin.ebay.com/ws/eBayISAPI.dll?SignIn&UsingSSL=1 &pUserId=?UPdate

--------Please do not reply to this message--------

eBay Support team
http://www.eBay.com

Figure 6-1. Phishing emails take many forms, but they usually have the official eBay logo on them and a very authentic-looking link. HTML in the email allows scammers to display an actual eBay link but invisibly embed a completely different web address—so when you click the link, you'll go to a fake web page designed to dupe you into giving out personal information.

People always take it personally, as though the scammer had *their* address and targeted them specifically, but that's not how it works. Like spammers, phishers often purchase enormous lists of email addresses and send the same email to everyone—without knowing whether they have an eBay account or not. I've also gotten phishing emails purportedly from Washington Mutual and Citibank. Both said my account would be suspended, which didn't exactly put the fear of God into me since I don't even *have* an account with either company.

> **NOTE**   If you aren't sure an email supposedly from eBay or
> PayPal is real, forward it (with full headers, when
> possible) to *spoof@ebay.com* or *spoof@paypal.com*.
> You'll receive a quick reply.

There's an old saying that goes, "Even a blind squirrel eventually finds a nut." That's the mindset of the phishers—send out enough emails and at least some will produce results.

Do a little math. If they send out a million emails and only one percent of the people who get them respond, that's 10,000 new identities to steal. Multiply that by untold numbers (since far more than a million phishing emails are sent every year), and you see why the scam is more than worth the effort.

Identity theft used to be hard work. It required sifting through strangers' trash, hoping to find an intact, legible credit card statement or other document with enough personal information to put together a profile of the person. Between the physical work required and the thieves' reluctance to muck through coffee grounds and cigarette butts with no guarantee of results, the problem wasn't terribly widespread.

But now? All that's required is a few computer keystrokes and a little patience. To say they have it down to a science would be a gross understatement.

> **WARNING**   Just because an email's return address has ebay.com in
> it doesn't mean it's actually from eBay. It's extremely
> easy to spoof (fake) email headers and addresses. In
> general, it's better not to click links in emails anyway—
> no matter how real the email or the link may appear.
> Use a trusted bookmark to reach a site instead, or type
> the site's front door URL (such as ebay.com) into the
> address bar of your browser yourself.

And sometimes it's not just your identity they're after, but your good name on eBay, too. If you give your eBay password to a thief, he now has the information he needs to hijack your account and list items for sale under your ID.

Why would he do that? To steal money, of course. The goal is to list an expensive item at a great price, get the buyer to wire money for payment, and disappear into the night—leaving *you* holding the bag.

Escape it!

If you've been duped into filling out one of those phony web forms, time is of the essence. You need to minimize or, hopefully, prevent any damage.

If you provided a credit card number, call your card company. You don't need to go into the whole embarrassing story with the customer service rep—simply state the card was lost. The old account numbers are then canceled (making them unusable) and a card with new numbers is issued to you.

Ditto if you gave out your bank account numbers. While it's much tougher to pull money from a bank account than to use a credit card belonging to someone else, a scammer could use your account number for other purposes. Don't even give him the chance.

Explain to your bank clerk that you're afraid your identity has been stolen. She'll close the old account, open a new one, and give you a new ATM card. Be sure to change your PIN too. Destroy (as in, shred) any checks with the old account number on them.

Next you should call the Big Three credit bureaus—TransUnion, Equifax, and Experian—and place a *fraud alert* (or *security alert*) on your reports. Until you remove it, no one should be able to open any new credit accounts in your name unless you're contacted via your home or cell phone. Creditors can ignore the fraud alert and issue credit anyway, but most won't.

Here are the numbers to call:

TransUnion: (800) 680-7289
Equifax: (800) 525-6285
Experian: (888) 397-3742

Spotting a Hijacked Account

Let's say you're browsing eBay one day and you come across a fantastic deal. The seller has a long history on eBay and terrific *feedback*. How do you know if what you're seeing is an honest listing or one posted as the result of an account takeover (a.k.a. hijacking)? Here are some things to look for.

Big item, little price, free shipping

Common sense is your best ally. Scammers know people on eBay are looking for a bargain, and they'll often list something hoping to tap into our sense of greed. I've seen cars, tractors, and plasma TVs (a particular scammer favorite) listed for a fraction of their retail price, and the auction description offered free delivery to boot. Was the seller inexperienced or stupid? His feedback didn't indicate either one, so the logical conclusion is the account had been taken over by a hijacker.

Different contact information

Something else to look for is a notation in the auction that the email address attached to the seller's eBay account is "down." The auction description will ask potential buyers to contact the seller through an alternative address rather than using the "ask seller a question" button (which sends your question to the email address on file for the account).

Scammers want you to email them directly because they don't want to alert the actual account holder of what's going on. You may think a hijacker would avoid the problem by changing all the account information, but actually the opposite is true. Altering an email address or a password triggers a confirmation email to the account holder, and that's the last thing a hijacker wants. He wants to get in and get out quickly, silently, and with a minimum of attention. A perfect hijack is never detected while it's taking place.

So in order to avoid alerting the account holder, the hijacker puts an email address in the auction description. It's usually an address from Yahoo, Hotmail, etc.—something that can be used and easily discarded.

Needless to say, you should always use the features eBay has in place to email a seller rather than the address in an auction description.

—continued—

Which one of these is not like the others?

Finally, you can check a seller's other auctions (or her closed auctions) to see if they're similar to that big-ticket item. I once spotted a hijacker simply by noticing the seller normally sold trinkets like crystal kittens and porcelain figurines—so chances were good she wasn't suddenly making a foray into large farm equipment.

Prior (or current) auctions also show you how the seller lists her items. Does she use an auction template? A background color? A font different than the default Times Roman? Auctions from the same seller usually have a consistent look, so one that appears radically different than the others may be a sign that something's amiss.

Be a good samaritan

If you see an auction you believe is the result of an account hijacking, eBay has a special way to report it.

Go to *http://pages.ebay.com/help/contact_inline/account_security. html* and select the following choices in the corresponding fields.

1. Report fake emails (spoofs) and unauthorized account activity
2. Unauthorized account activity (account security issues)
3. Report another person's account as stolen
4. Click Continue, and then use the "email" link to detail your suspicions

eBay takes account theft very seriously so these reports are investigated quickly. If action is required, it's immediate—the phony auction is pulled and the seller's account suspended until the mess is sorted out.

NOTE   As of April 2003, calling just one credit bureau is supposedly sufficient. It then electronically alerts the other bureaus of your request to have a fraud alert placed on your reports. But it still wouldn't hurt to call all three, just in case.

Once you request the fraud alert, you'll be opted out of pre-approved credit card and insurance offers for two years. You'll also receive a free copy of your credit report (be sure to request it).

Each alert stays on your report until you remove it or for a maximum period of time, which varies depending on the credit bureau: 3 months for Experian, 6 months for Equifax, and 12 months for TransUnion. When they expire, you'll need to call if you want them renewed.

If accounts have already been opened in your name, you should immediately file a police report and request a copy. Having it in hand makes getting fraudulent information removed from your credit reports much easier. Check out the Fight Identity Theft web page (Figure 6-2) for more on this.

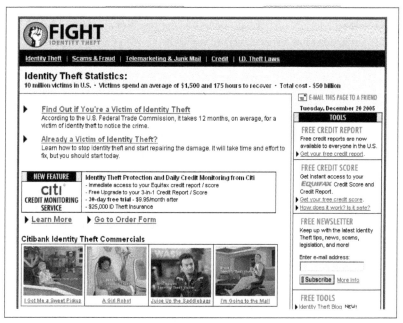

Figure 6-2. For more information on avoiding and dealing with identity theft, visit http://www.fightidentitytheft.com.

Now, if it's just your eBay information the scammers were after, mitigating the damage is a bit easier.

Login to your eBay account and check your My eBay page. If your username has bid on or listed anything for sale recently, it's shown there.

If all's well (in other words, no auctions you don't recognize as your own or bids you didn't place), you'll probably just need to change your password. On the left side of your My eBay page, look for My Account, and then click Personal Information. Click the Edit link next to your password and follow the instructions for changing it (see Figure 6-3).

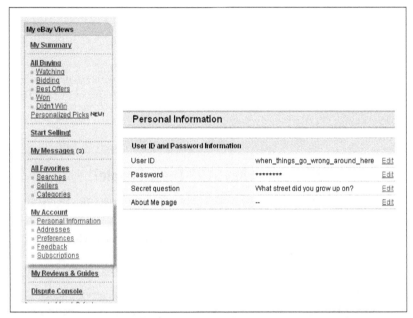

Figure 6-3. The Personal Information section of your My eBay page. When you change things, eBay sends an email to your address on file—you'll need to click the link in it for the changes to take effect.

If you login to your account and find auctions you didn't post or bids that aren't your doing, you'll need to report this to eBay at *http:// pages.ebay.com/help/tp/isgw-account-theft-reporting.html*. On that page you'll also find a special *Live Help* link (Figure 6-4) specifically for victims of account theft.

Contacting eBay

If you are unable to <u>sign in</u> to your eBay account, or if you require additional assistance, contact us immediately through Live Help.

<D> <u>Live help</u>

Note: If you have installed a pop-up or ad blocker, this software may interfere with Live Help. To use Live Help, turn off pop-up or ad blocking and refresh the page.

If you cannot use Live Help:

- <u>Email us</u> to report that you cannot sign in to your account.
- <u>Email us</u> after signing in to your account to request additional assistance.

Figure 6-4. The Account Theft page has a Live Help link that allows you to immediately chat with an eBay rep. This is different from the regular Live Help link on the main eBay.com home page and should be used only for Account Theft emergencies.

Why Can't eBay STOP These People?!

The short answer is "because eBay has no control over international criminals."

Phishing isn't usually done by a couple of college kids on a whim. It's far more complicated than that. It involves huge rings of extremely skilled hackers and programmers, most of them outside the U.S.

eBay user (and Answer Center regular) fatiguee provides an excellent and a very thorough explanation at *http://answercenter.ebay.com/thread. jsp?forum=2&thread=810062587*.

Second-Chance Offer Scams

Judy bid on a Stradivarius violin worth several thousand dollars. She was eventually outbid, but moments after the auction closed, she received an email from the seller with a *Second Chance Offer* (SCO).

He told Judy the winner backed out, so the violin was hers if she wanted it at her high bid amount. He then requested payment via Western Union wire transfer. Judy asked to pay via PayPal as the auction stated she could, but the seller said something was wrong with his PayPal account and until it was straightened out, he could accept money only via WU.

This sounded plausible to Judy because she had recently had a problem with PayPal herself, so she did as the seller requested and wired payment to him.

A couple of weeks later, wondering why she hadn't yet received her violin, she emailed the seller but the email bounced back to her as undeliverable. She then went to the auction page, clicked on the seller's name and then the "contact member" button, thinking perhaps the seller had changed his email address.

She got a reply a short time later. The seller, whose name and email address were different than those of the person who'd originally contacted her, had no idea what Judy was talking about. He'd completed the auction with the original winner and they'd already left feedback for each other.

Judy was sure he'd scammed her but with no proof, she was out of luck—and thousands of dollars poorer.

Avoid it!

Judy fell victim to an SCO scam. Here's how they work.

Scammers troll the bid histories of big-ticket auctions to look for bidders they may be able to dupe (eBay newbies are a particular favorite). After the auction closes, they contact their victims through the eBay system using the "contact member" feature.

The scammers represent themselves as the seller and typically claim the winner of the auction backed out. They then offer the pricey item to the underbidder but insist on a WU payment. (Even though the username on the initial email is different than the seller's, most people don't seem to notice, so crazed are they to get their hands on the item they lost out on.)

The scammers often contact more than one of the underbidders in an effort to rob several people at once, but they need only one person to follow through for the ruse to be immensely profitable.

SCO scams started popping up almost as soon as eBay introduced the SCO feature (those pesky scammers never sleep). Used properly, the SCO is a great way for a seller to offer an item to an underbidder without having to pay to relist it. She can do this if the winner bails on her, if she has multiples of the item she's selling, or if the bidding doesn't reach a reserve in a *Reserve Price auction*.

Real SCOs trigger an eBay-generated email with a link to the SCO auction page. That page is also system-generated, meaning the seller can change nothing on it.

It will look identical to the original auction (same photos, same description, and same payment terms) except it'll have a Buy It Now price in the amount of the underbidder's highest bid amount. The SCO auction can't be found using eBay's search engines, and the only person who can use the BIN is the bidder who received the SCO.

Now, this is the most important thing to know: *SCOs are NEVER conducted through email*. They operate just as any other BIN auction does: click the BIN button to purchase the item, and pay using one of the methods detailed in the auction.

By doing this, you're staying within the safe (or at least safer) confines of eBay. You can exchange feedback for the transaction and eBay and/or PayPal will get involved if there's a problem.

SCO scammers want to keep you far away from eBay and the actual auction. Sometimes they'll even offer an oh-so-generous discount off your bid price if you pay within 24 hours. They don't want to give you time to think or investigate. They'll tell you whatever's necessary to get you to follow through, and they'll lie relentlessly.

Once they've gotten what they want, they'll disappear along with your money. You'll think the original seller scammed you, but he's almost never involved.

The Hallmarks of a Real SCO

If your eyes are glazing over while reading the fine details, just remember all three of these conditions must apply:

You receive an email from eBay referring to a Second Chance Offer in the subject line. The email *never* has a subject line that reads, "Question from eBay Member." Those emails are generic questions that can be sent by anyone who stumbled across your username and used the "contact member" button on your profile page.

The email has a link to a Buy It Now auction. All the information on it, including the photographs, description, payment terms, and the seller's ID match the original auction. The eBay system doesn't allow the seller to change anything. As soon as he extends the SCO, eBay automatically generates the SCO auction page and emails you. Never pay for anything unless your name is listed as the winner of a closed auction.

The SCO is on your My eBay page. Under the heading "Items I Didn't Win," you see the original auction and a highlighted bar under it that says you got an SCO (with a link to the SCO auction page).

Still not convinced that what you're seeing is real? Email the seller using the "contact member" feature on his feedback page. Your note goes to the email address eBay has on file for the actual seller, who can reply to you either directly or through the eBay system.

Above all: never pay for any eBay item using a Western Union wire transfer! (see Chapter 2 for more on that).

I've heard people scream about SCO scams and demand eBay do something about them, but what is there to do? To stop phony SCOs, eBay would have to either remove the SCO feature (which is really quite handy when used properly) or remove members' ability to contact each other.

Instead they've put into place a secure system to keep you from being scammed, but you must stay within the confines of eBay. Stray outside it and you're on your own.

> **N O T E**   If you'd rather not be contacted with even legitimate
> SCOs, you can opt out by going to your My eBay
> page, and then to My Account → Preferences. Under
> Buying Notifications, uncheck the box next to "Sec-
> ond Chance Offer emails," then scroll down and
> click the Save button. By doing this you may be giv-
> ing up the opportunity to get that groovy macraméd
> purse on which you were outbid, but at least you'll
> know any SCO you get is fake.

Escape it!

Depending on how far into the scam you've been pulled, you may be
able to back out in time. Just stop replying to the scammer's emails
and eventually he'll move on to someone he can actually sucker.

> **N O T E**   Any time you receive an email from another eBay
> member in which an offer to buy or sell outside of
> eBay is proposed, you should report it at Help →
> Contact Us → Report Problems With Other eBay
> Members.

If you've already wired your money, I'm sorry to say there's not
much that can be done. Right at the top of any email you receive
from other eBay members is a big warning about the dangers of purchasing items outside of eBay or using Western Union to pay for
them.

If you refuse to protect yourself, there's not much eBay can do to
protect you either.

Web of Lies

For years, my friends and I have joked, "I saw it on the Internet. It
must be true." Snarky sarcasm aside, be aware that web sites are
transient little beasts: what's here today can be long gone tomorrow.

All Escrow Sites Aren't Created Equal

Lyle bid on a gorgeous diamond engagement ring for his fiancée but was subsequently outbid. After the auction closed, the newbie seller contacted him with a legitimate Second Chance Offer but said she hadn't yet had the opportunity to set up her PayPal account. She then asked for payment via Western Union.

Lyle had heard WU payments were a bad idea but the ring was so perfect that he asked the seller if there was any other method by which he could pay. The seller said she understood Lyle's concerns and offered to use an *escrow* service to put his mind at ease.

She gave him the web address of an escrow site she said she'd used many times before. Lyle visited the professional-looking site and was impressed. He emailed the company's accounting department directly and was told that once he wired payment, he would be sent the ring—and his money wouldn't be released to the seller until he notified the escrow service the ring had been received.

This sounded very safe, so Lyle wired money to the escrow company.

Two weeks later, having received nothing from either the seller or the escrow service, he returned to the escrow site—only to find it gone. The seller's eBay account had been suspended as well.

Avoid it!

Escrow scams can take several forms. Some of them are perpetrated by account hijackers (who can send official SCOs from the stolen username), some by new eBayers, and still others defraud through phony SCOs.

As with many scams, the seller claims PayPal trouble and asks for a wired WU payment. If you fall for that, her work is done. As I've told you over and over throughout this book, wired funds can be picked up anywhere in the world and are unrecoverable, so if she's able to steal your money that way, all the better for her.

But thieves realize many eBayers are hip to the WU scam now, so they've created an additional layer designed to garner trust: they offer to use an escrow service.

Phony escrow sites are simple to set up. All someone has to do is register an official-sounding domain and put up a few pages of text intended to convince you to use the "service."

Most of the phony sites I've run across look the same because similar templates are used over and over again. Sometimes they even get sloppy and leave the name of the last fake site in the new site's text.

A quick check of the domain information for these sites showed someone registered them very recently (usually someone outside the U.S.) and the sites were hosted on foreign servers.

The physical address given by the registrant is always phony. One was an empty storefront in South Africa. Another address didn't exist at all. But my favorite was the registrant who used the street address of Buckingham Palace (ah, those wacky royals).

So how can you protect yourself from this? Simple. If you're going to use an escrow service, there's only one in the U.S. endorsed by eBay, and the name is easier than a drunken Hilton sister: Escrow.com.

NOTE   eBay maintains a list of approved international escrow sites at *http://pages.ebay.com/help/confidence/payment-escrow.html*.

Once you suggest Escrow.com to a scammer, she'll either disappear or spew forth wildly absurd reasons why she doesn't want to use it. The most laughable one I've heard was the site "takes too long to pay sellers." In my experience, Escrow.com (see Figure 6-5) wires payment to my bank account just a couple of hours after a transaction is complete.

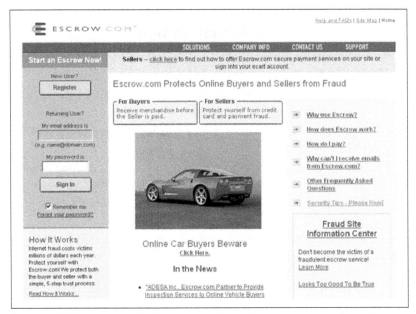

Figure 6-5. The homepage for Escrow.com, the only escrow service endorsed by eBay. Use another service at your peril.

Escape it!

As with any other WU scam, there isn't much hope of getting your money back. The scammers, even if identified, are almost always overseas and out of the reach of U.S. law enforcement.

Just because they're out of reach doesn't mean you shouldn't report them. Sites like FraudAid.com help you contact the appropriate authorities and write a complaint. It's also a great resource for news and information. Maybe your scammers haven't been caught yet, but you can cackle with glee at those who have.

The Magical, Mythical eBay Warehouse

Kari bid on but lost an auction for an expensive cell phone. Shortly afterwards she received an email from another eBay member, who said he had one of the phones if she wanted it. The only problem, it seemed, was that his monthly payment limit for PayPal was maxed out, so he could accept payment only via Western Union.

How Does Escrow Work?

An escrow service is essentially a "middle man" both parties can trust. Here's the order of a typical transaction:

1. The buyer and seller agree on the terms of the sale, including item description, selling price, and period of inspection.
2. The buyer pays the escrow service by check, money order, credit card, or wire transfer.
3. The seller ships the item to the buyer and provides tracking information to the escrow service so delivery can be verified.
4. The buyer inspects the merchandise and then either accepts or rejects it.
5. If the item is accepted, the seller is then paid via check or wire transfer. If the item is rejected, it's sent back to the seller. Once she verifies the item is in satisfactory condition, the buyer's money is refunded by the escrow service.

That's it. No muss, no fuss, and both parties are protected *if* you use a legitimate service like Escrow.com. Read the "How It Works" section of their site for more information.

He told Kari he had $5,000 in "purchase protection" from Square Trade, so there was no risk to her. If she didn't like the phone for any reason, she could return it to the eBay warehouse within five days of receiving it and ST would refund her money.

He directed her to a web site with ST in the name, and she later received emails from the site and from an eBay.com address. Both vouched for the seller's trustworthiness and encouraged Kari to complete the transaction.

Satisfied she was protected, Kari wired the money to the seller and awaited the arrival of her new toy. When weeks passed with no delivery, she contacted ST and asked for a refund. ST, however, had nothing to do with the transaction, and the eBay account of the person she paid was suspended.

Kari's money was gone.

Avoid it!

If Kari had done even the most basic of investigations, she'd have learned Square Trade is merely a third-party mediation service. It's not a division of eBay, nor does it facilitate transactions, provide escrow services, or vouch for anyone's credibility in the manner described.

Scammers latched onto the ST name at some point, probably because eBay used to be heavily affiliated with the site. ST simply mediated disputes about feedback and such, and for a while they even had the pull to get eBay to completely remove negative feedback. (That stopped happening in early 2004—now ST can just recommend the feedback be withdrawn.)

Like fake escrow sites, there are a *lot* of fake ST sites out there floating around in the dark corners of cyberspace. The official site is *http://www.squaretrade.com*, but the phonies usually have the ST name in them so they sound authentic.

The creation of the "eBay warehouse" is relatively new. It's usually used in scams to indicate eBay's involvement in what the thief is doing. He may say an expensive car he's trying to get you to pay for is being housed there, or, as in Kari's story, that the warehouse is where unwanted items should be returned.

It's also where leprechauns and unicorns frolic together in a state of bliss. It's a magical place, I tell you!

Just don't try to find it. It doesn't exist, except in the imaginations of crooks and thieves. And like ST, eBay doesn't vouch for anyone's trustworthiness (the emails Kari got had spoofed return addresses). I can't even imagine what would happen if you tried to send them an item you wanted to return.

Kari's story is just one of the many incarnations the ST/warehouse scam has taken. It changes a bit every time I see it, as it's highly adaptable to a scammer's whims and a victim's gullibility.

> NOTE   eBay user ArielMT2's "Me" page has lots of fantastic
> information to keep both buyers and sellers from
> being scammed (including Jenny_Lake's famous-on-
> the-forums missive, "The Thirteen Red Flags of
> Fraud"). Read it all at *http://members.ebay.com/
> aboutme/arielmt2*.

But really, Kari's involvement should've stopped before it began. Once she received that unsolicited email from someone trying to get her to purchase something outside of eBay, she should have reported it and walked away.

There's a reason eBay has rules about those things. They're trying to protect the unwashed masses from making impoverished fools of themselves.

Escape it!

Yet another WU scam (though it certainly doesn't own the scammer market). Have I taught you nothing? Report it as indicated earlier in this chapter.

And please, be safe out there.

The Switcheroo Scam

Think back to your childhood, when your big sister would distract you by excitedly exclaiming, "Look! A puppy!", only to quickly swap her half-eaten cake for your larger slice. This is sort of like that, but worse.

Know Your Item

Mitch sold a rare miniature of a classic car, *mint* in the pristine box. His buyer paid via PayPal and he shipped the item to her.

A week later, she emailed Mitch and said the car and box had damage undisclosed in the auction and she wanted to return it for a refund. He was surprised but since he wanted to keep his customer happy, he agreed to a refund upon the item's return.

When he got it back, it was a mess. The box was old and dusty, and the car inside had clearly been played with many times.

Mitch told his buyer this wasn't the item he sent her but she insisted it was—and when she didn't immediately get a refund, she filed a complaint with PayPal.

Avoid it!

This is what's commonly known as "the old switcheroo."

Here's how it works: the buyer has an item she'd like to replace but she doesn't want to spend the money to do so. She checks eBay, finds an exact match of her item in brand-new condition, and purchases it. Upon receiving the new item, she claims it has damage the auction didn't specify so she wants to return it. She then sends back her old item for a refund while keeping the new one for herself.

If the seller falls for the scam and refunds her money, the buyer winds up with the new item *and* her money back.

The switcheroo scam seems to be perpetrated most often against sellers of computer equipment and other electronics. If you compare two PC memory cards with the same make and model, you'll find they usually look identical. So a person who's somehow ruined the one they have may be able to easily pull off a switcheroo and replace it for free. It can also be done with CD players, DVD players, etc.

So what's a seller to do? The solution may be easier than you think.

The vast majority (if not all) of electronic items have an individual serial number—sometimes it's stamped or etched right onto the item itself, and sometimes the number is on a sticker. But the number for each item is completely unique.

Sellers should photograph and write down the serial numbers of the items they're selling, and keep them someplace safe. That way if a buyer tries to pull a switcheroo, the seller knows since the serial number he's documented for the item doesn't match the one on the returned item.

NOTE   Some sellers even put a photo of the serial number right into the auction. This dissuades scammers from purchasing the item in the first place, and provides evidence of the number in the event of a PayPal dispute.

Now, what about items that don't have serial numbers?

The method of proving a switcheroo is less exact for them but some sellers swear by it: get a pen with so-called "invisible ink" (it's actually ink that only shows up under a blacklight) and discretely put a unique mark on each item that goes out. Sellers who do this check returned items for the mark before agreeing to refund.

Other sellers do nothing at all except rely on plain old bravado—if a buyer claims an item was misrepresented and she wants to return it, the seller sweetly replies, "Okay, no problem. When I get it back, I'll check it for my unique mark to make sure the item is mine. Once I determine it is, I'll be happy to refund you."

Some sellers mark the items, some don't—but according to many of them, just sending that note makes most of the suspicious buyers go away, never to be heard from again. The general consensus is that buyers who agree to return the item anyway are usually on the up and up.

Foolproof? No. But apparently effective nonetheless.

Escape it!

What to do, what to do.

Well, let's get the easy one out of the way first. If a buyer paid with a method *other* than PayPal, sellers have more choices regarding whether to refund or not.

I say that with some trepidation because I don't want sellers to think they can get away with misrepresenting items. As I detail in Chapter 2, that's just not true—there are many resources available to buyers who've been duped.

But the fact remains that PayPal's arms are long and thus much more capable of squeezing refunds out of sellers. It's one reason so many buyers prefer to pay with PayPal—they get protections some other methods of payment don't provide.

Ironically, a buyer trying to scam a new item out of a seller usually pays using PayPal precisely *because* of its buyer protection. A double-edged sword, that.

But just because a buyer files a claim doesn't mean she'll win. The claims process often includes what PayPal calls a Dispute Resolution Specialist—a fancy term for the PayPal rep who listens to both sides of the dispute and decides who should prevail.

To view PayPal's Resolution Center Tutorials, log in to Paypal, click the Resolution Center link at the top, and then click Resolution Center Tutorials (see Figure 6-6).

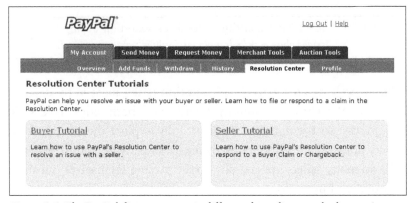

Figure 6-6. The PayPal dispute process is different depending on whether you're a buyer or a seller. View the tutorials for both so you'll know what to expect.

The good part of having an actual human involved is that documentation can be submitted and examined. So if we use Mitch in our story as an example, he could submit photos of the item he sent (presumably they would be the same ones he had on the auction) and photos of the item that was returned to him to demonstrate the enormous difference. Sellers with evidence of serial number discrepancies can submit those as well.

Sometimes the Dispute Resolution Specialist's job comes down to the simple question of which party is most credible. What exactly he examines to determine this isn't documented publicly, but logic dictates it would probably include things like each person's record with PayPal and/or eBay, the manner in which both people communicate with the Specialist, the evidence each provides, etc.

So if you're a seller and you feel a scamming buyer is victimizing you, don't just roll over, play dead, and issue a refund. Fight back. PayPal may provide a lot of protection to buyers, but it does take measures to ensure that protection isn't blatantly abused.

One final note here... many long-time sellers refuse to leave feedback before a buyer does because of situations like this. Although "feedback extortion" (as it's called on eBay) isn't allowed, some buyers who've already received glowing feedback from their sellers use it as leverage when trying to get an unjustified refund.

NOTE   Read what constitutes feedback extortion at *http://pages.ebay.com/help/policies/feedback-extortion.html*.

The "who leaves feedback first" question is the most hotly debated topic on the eBay Community boards and both sides have valid arguments, so I won't even begin to fully explore the issue here (it could almost fill an entire book by itself). I just want you to be aware why so many sellers are gun-shy about putting themselves out there before their buyers do.

Glossary

The terms in this glossary are briefly explained. eBay keeps a comprehensive glossary at *http://pages.ebay.com/help/newtoebay/glossary.html*.

Address Confirmation

A PayPal process whereby the buyer submits a credit card and PayPal matches up the card's billing address to the mailing address the buyer submitted when he opened up his PayPal account.

Advanced Search Page

The page on eBay where you can do more detailed searches for auctions (including those that have already ended), as well as searches on the activity of buyers and sellers.

Answer Center

A forum in the Community section of eBay. As opposed to the Discussion Boards in the same section, the AC is for quick questions and answers (each thread is limited to 10 replies).

Bid cancellation

A process by which a *seller* cancels an existing bid on an active auction.

Bid history

The page showing all the bids on an auction. To access it, click the hyperlinked number (e.g., "13 bids") on the *auction* page.

Bid increment

The set amount a bid is raised every time the current bid is exceeded. Increments are based on the *current* high bid (view the bid increment chart at *http://pages.ebay.com/help/buy/bid-increments.html*).

Bid retraction

The process by which a *bidder* rescinds his bid(s) on an active auction.

Bid Shielding

Two or more bidders deliberately raising the price of an item to extremely high levels in order to scare other bidders away, and then retracting most of the bids at the last second. This enabled one of the bidders to win the item at an artificially low price. The 12-Hour Rule pretty much eliminated the ability to do this.

Bidding war

Two or more people placing numerous bids on the same auction.

Blocked Bidder List (BBL)

Allows a seller to prohibit designated users from bidding on her auctions.

Buy It Now (BIN)

The price for which a seller is willing to sell the item immediately. If a seller wishes to designate a BIN price, it will be at the top of an auction page, NOT in the item description.

Buyer Protection Policy (BPP)

PayPal's policies that ensure a buyer gets what he paid for.

Buyer Block Exemption List (BBEL)

Allows a seller to designate certain bidders as exempt from rules set in her Seller Preferences (permits a foreign bidder to bid on a U.S.-only auction, etc.).

Complaint of Non-receipt

A report filed by a buyer with eBay and/or PayPal stating an item has been paid for and not received.

Contact Member (feature)

Allows eBay users to contact each other without needing an email address to do so. The Contact Member button is on each user's profile page (which can be accessed by clicking on the feedback number next to his user-name).

Delivery Confirmation (DC)

An extra service from the USPS that shows the date, time and zip code to which the item was delivered.

Dispute Console

The page where eBay users can see any ongoing disputes in which they're involved and reply to them.

eBay Trading Assistant

Someone who, for a fee, will sell items on eBay for you.

Escrow

Appointing a "middle man" to ensure a buyer receives his item and a seller receives the money for it. Usually used only for very expensive items.

Fee Avoidance

The act of a seller intentionally avoiding eBay fees. Also called "fee circumvention."

Feedback

Comments left for each other by buyers and sellers who have been in a transaction together.

Feedback Score

The total number of positive comments a user has accrued. It may be expressed as a number or a percentage.

Final Value Fees (FVF)

The percentage eBay takes of an auction's final selling price.

Global Express Guaranteed (GXE)

A method of shipping internationally through the USPS that

allows tracking the package in transit.

Hidden proxy or high proxy

The highest amount a bidder is willing to pay for the item at the time the bid is placed. The eBay system uses only the portion of it necessary to keep her in the lead, and the rest of the proxy is hidden from other users until and unless it is exceeded by another bid.

High bidder

The person who bid more than other bidders.

Hijacked account

An eBay account that has been taken over by someone who probably fooled the account owner into giving away the information necessary to gain access.

ID

Another term for an eBay username.

Item Not Received/Significantly Not As Described (INR/SNAD)

The eBay process that allows a buyer to report an item paid for has not been received or isn't what was described in the auction.

Listing

Another word for auction, or the process of putting an auction on eBay.

Listing fees

The amount eBay charges a seller to put an auction on its site.

Live bid

A bid on an auction that has not yet ended.

Live Help

eBay's "chat" system that allows users to immediately speak with an eBay representative.

Local Pick-up

An auction designation that means the seller will not ship the item, so the buyer will have to pick it up himself.

Mint

An auction adjective that means an item is perfect, unblemished and/or like new. Items that are said to be "mint in box" are often described with the acronym MIB.

Mutual Feedback Withdrawal (MFW)

The process that allows two users who have already left feedback for each other to "neutralize" the impact of it on their overall feedback scores. The comments left by both will remain in their respective feedback profiles.

My eBay page

The page each user has that allows tracking and managing of buying/selling activity, account information, messaging, preferences, etc.

Not a Registered User (NARU)

The designation given to a user eBay has barred from using the site.

Negative feedback

The comments one user leaves for another when she's unhappy

with a transaction. Negative feedback deducts points from the recipient's overall feedback score.

Negged/negging

The act of leaving negative feedback for another eBay user.

Neutral feedback

If a user is neither happy nor unhappy with a transaction, he may leave neutral feedback instead. It does not affect on the recipient's overall feedback score.

Newbie

Someone new to eBay.

Non-paying Bidder (NPB)

A buyer who does not pay for the items he won.

Non-performing Seller Report

The report a buyer can file with eBay if a seller refuses to sell her the item she won.

Online DC

Electronically issued USPS Delivery Confirmation.

PayPal

Payment service used by most eBayers.

Phishing

The act of sending fraudulent emails in which the sender claims to be a legitimate company/ entity and attempts to trick the recipient into surrendering personal information. The information is used for identity theft or to hijack an eBay account.

Priority Mail

The class of USPS mail typically delivered in 2-3 business days.

Private auction

An auction in which the list of bidders is hidden from public view.

Proxy

The highest amount a bidder is willing to pay for the item at the time the bid is placed. The eBay system uses only the portion of it necessary to keep her in the lead, and the rest is hidden from other users.

Registered Mail

The most secure way to ship through the USPS.

Reserve Price auction

An auction in which a seller has set an amount under which he's not obligated to sell.

Retail DC

USPS Delivery Confirmation purchased at the post office.

Second Chance Offer (SCO)

After an auction closes, this allows a seller to offer identical items to one or more of the losing bidders for their highest bid amount.

Sell Your Item (SYI)

The pages eBay sellers fill out to list an auction.

Seller Preferences

A set of criteria eBay sellers select limiting who can bid on their auctions.

Seller Protection Policy (SPP)

PayPal's policies to protect sellers against fraud.

Shill Bidding or Shilling

The act of a seller raising the price of his own auctions by using another ID to bid on them himself or having a friend/family member bid on them.

Sniping

Placing bids in the final minutes or seconds of an auction.

Spam

Unsolicited email.

Square Trade

A third-party mediation service sometimes used by eBayers.

Standard Purchase Protection Program (SPPP)

eBay policy that reimburses buyers a limited amount if they do not receive what they paid for or it is significantly not as described in the auction.

Strike removal

The act of a seller removing a previously issued non-paying bidder strike (usually because the buyer paid and the seller accepted payment).

Suspension of Account (Suspension Notice)

The email eBay sends when an account has been suspended from using the site.

Time and date stamp

The system mark eBay puts on auctions (showing when they were listed) and bids (showing when they were placed). Time stamps are always shown in Pacific Time.

Terms of Sale/Service (TOS)

The conditions a seller puts in his auctions. Includes method of shipment, shipping and handling fees, etc.

Tracking number

A number assigned to a package that may show where it is in transit, and always shows when it has been delivered.

Transaction interference

The eBay policy that prohibits warning someone away from an item or a seller. It also prohibits bidders from asking a seller to sell an item outside of eBay.

12-Hour Rule

eBay's policy that restricts certain activities by bidders or a seller when his auction is in its final 12 hours.

Underbidder

Someone who bid on an auction but was not the highest bidder when it closed.

Uniform Commercial Code (UCC)

A set of laws governing commercial transactions.

Unpaid Item Report (UPI)

The report filed by sellers against non-paying bidders.

Unpaid Item Strike (UIS)

Issued to non-paying bidders by sellers who file and later close UPIs.

Username

Another term for the name someone uses on eBay.

Verified Rights Owner (VeRO)

An eBay body comprised of intellectual property rights owners empowered to report and request removal of listings that infringe upon their rights.

Watch list

Located on your My eBay page, this is the list of auctions you've marked to watch.

Winning proxy bid

The highest bid showing at the end of an auction.

Index

We'd like to hear your suggestions for improving our indexes. Send email to *index@oreilly.com*.

S

About the Author

Shauna Wright has been writing since she was old enough to put pencil to paper. Much to her dismay, her mother still has the mock "newscast" she wrote when she was eight (which included a reference to Walter Croncat—no, that's not a typo).

She holds a bachelor's degree in criminology from the University of Memphis, where she was the president of the Pre-Law Society for two years and participated in other student government groups. She balanced this with copious social time as the "little sister" of a campus fraternity, the members of which probably still remember her as the girl who hated beer.

Shauna signed up with eBay in 1998 and has bought and sold everything from clothes to cosmetics to far less girly items like computer hardware. Her background in criminology taught her to be suspicious of everyone, so she's exerted much energy learning to protect herself and others from being ripped off. Time permitting, she shares her knowledge (and paranoia) on eBay's Answer Center boards.

Over the years she's been a speaker at many web conferences, lecturing about such topics as writing for the Web, information design, and dealing with difficult clients. She's written on sites such as Fray.com, Teen-Wire.com, and a whole bunch that aren't around anymore. She's the co-founder of WhoWouldBuyThat.com, which gives her a much-needed outlet for snark.

She's an avid fan of *The Daily Show*, TelevisionWithoutPity.com, Lyle Lovett, and anything Aaron Sorkin has ever done. She believes in karma and is always kind to animals and the elderly. Her boyfriend says she's "built like that girl on the mudflaps," and she loves him for it.

Colophon

The cover image for *Don't Get Burned on eBay* is from the CMCD Everyday Objects collection. The cover font is Adobe ITC Garamond. The text font is Linotype Birka; the heading font is Adobe Myriad Condensed; and the code font is LucasFont's TheSans Mono Condensed.

Get even more for your money.

Join the O'Reilly Community, and register the O'Reilly books you own. It's free, and you'll get:

- $4.99 ebook upgrade offer
- 40% upgrade offer on O'Reilly print books
- Membership discounts on books and events
- Free lifetime updates to ebooks and videos
- Multiple ebook formats, DRM FREE
- Participation in the O'Reilly community
- Newsletters
- Account management
- 100% Satisfaction Guarantee

Signing up is easy:

1. **Go to: oreilly.com/go/register**
2. **Create an O'Reilly login.**
3. **Provide your address.**
4. **Register your books.**

Note: English-language books only

To order books online:

oreilly.com/store

For questions about products or an order:

orders@oreilly.com

To sign up to get topic-specific email announcements and/or news about upcoming books, conferences, special offers, and new technologies:

elists@oreilly.com

For technical questions about book content:

booktech@oreilly.com

To submit new book proposals to our editors:

proposals@oreilly.com

O'Reilly books are available in multiple DRM-free ebook formats. For more information:

oreilly.com/ebooks

O'REILLY®

Spreading the knowledge of innovators · oreilly.com

Have it your way.